Sticks and Stones

Sticks and Stones

7 Ways Your Child Can Deal with Teasing, Conflict, and Other Hard Times

SCOTT COOPER

TIMES BOOKS
RANDOM HOUSE

 Published in the United States by Times Books, a division of Random House, Inc., New York, and simultaneously in Canada by Random House of Canada Limited, Toronto.

Library of Congress Cataloging-in-Publication data is available

ISBN 0-8129-3240-4

Random House website address: www.randomhouse.com

Printed in the United States of America on acid-free paper

98765432

Book design by Maura Fadden Rosenthal
Illustrations by Ed Lam

To Adam, Jackson, and Brooke with all my love.

In loving memory of Katie, who is always with us.

ACKNOWLEDGMENTS

A little over twenty years ago, when I was going to college and also teaching in a private school, I first thumbed through the simple, little book *When I Say No, I Feel Guilty,* by Manuel J. Smith. His tools enabled me to immediately help some of my students and were also good for me personally. Over the years, as I've surveyed the landscape for additional tools of communication and assertiveness training, I've found few tools that have significantly improved on his simple system. I'm grateful for his influence. I'm also grateful for the thinking and writings of Jon Kabat-Zinn and Dr. David Burns, both of whom are referenced in this book, in the realms of mindfulness and cognitive therapy.

I'm grateful to Times Books and especially to Betsy Rapoport. Not only is she a great editor, she's a great person. I wish all writers could experience her level of professionalism, support, and kindness. Also thanks to Mary Beth Roche, Kate Larkin, Martha Schwartz, Mindy Schultz, and others for their kind help. Thanks to Mary Anne Smith for her wonderful cover design.

Special thanks to Gary Diedrichs, who was instrumental in helping me to refine portions of early drafts of my book.

I was fortunate to have grown up as the youngest person in a great family. My own parents, brothers, and sisters provided me with exceptional examples of what good parenting looks like. I'll always be grateful for their positive influence.

Saving the best for last, I'm deeply appreciative of my wife, Julie, for her daily example of good parenting and good communication. In addition to her reviewing my writing several times and giving no-holds-barred, honest opinions (which only a spouse can give), I've stolen some of her thinking and approaches for this book. She's not only the love of my life, she's the best parent that I've personally been acquainted with.

CONTENTS

Sticks and Stones

Some Background

A VERBAL TOOLBOX

Within the same moment I could feel my heart sink and my anger surge. Here was my seven-year-old son, his shoulders shaking and his big, brown eyes welling with tears, and he was looking up at me for help. My easy-going, "perfect" son had just been picked on by a belligerent bully, and I wasn't going to stand for it. Somebody would have to pay.

Fortunately, as I marched out the front door, I became aware of what was happening inside me and I calmed down. Actually, the belligerent bully didn't look very belligerent at all. In fact, he looked a lot like my neighbor's "perfect" son. I dealt with the situation without losing it and found out that my son hadn't been quite so perfect in this case. As it turned out, my son's feelings had spilled over and he had responded to his teasing neighbor friend with hitting and pushing—all natural little boy reactions. But the experience made me realize that I hadn't prepared my son to deal with these kinds of situations. For that matter, I hadn't taught him how to deal with hardly any kind of difficult social situation.

I began to realize in that moment that all of us carry around an internal toolbox. In that toolbox are all the tools we own for dealing with every sort of situation, confrontation, and human contact. If all I find in my toolbox when you threaten me is a hammer, I'll pound you with it. But if I also carry around lighter, more subtle tools, I'll have them available to try first. Kids need such tools, not just to deal with other kids but for the even bigger dilemma of dealing with adults—how do you tell an unkind or unfair adult to cut it out?

I decided that my son needed more than a hammer. Besides being his father, I had the background to give him something more. I had been blessed with a father who cared authentically about young people and dedicated his life to training them. As a high school agriculture teacher in the heart of the Napa Valley, he had taken many students (less academically inclined in some cases) and helped them hone their practical skills through on-the-job projects. Some of these young men would go on to become highly regarded practitioners in the wine industry. Maybe because of my father's influence, I had spent a lot of my own adult life interested and involved in youth development efforts. Initially I had been a bilingual aide, teacher, and coach. After I obtained an MBA and entered the business world, I maintained a strong connection with youth development by coaching and participating on school and drug prevention boards. Through the years I had researched and developed a few of my own tools to help kids in the areas of self-esteem, assertiveness, and conflict resolution—all areas that related to the tools I wanted my son to have. I had experimented in teaching these principles to teenagers and had a sense of what worked and what didn't.

Additionally, the business world had increased my awareness (if not enjoyment) of real-world confrontation and negotiation and the strategies for dealing with tough social situations.

Kids also need the skills to deal with us, their own parents, especially when, too distracted by the daily hustle and bustle, we forget to be kind and reasonable.

Failing in my search for a good one-stop resource that I could use to teach my son the tools I wanted him to have, I began to pull together my own past research and experience, and the experience of my wife, Julie, in a form that I could use to teach our three children. After trial and error, I arrived at a way of giving our children a set of useful verbal tools that could help them deal with a wide range of difficult social situations. My hope is that you won't have to go through the same long process to find these helpful tools.

As parents we know that the childhood saying about sticks and stones isn't always true. Sticks and stones certainly hurt and so can names and words. The main point of *Sticks and Stones* is to give your children the verbal tools to counter the hurtful words others tell them and that they tell themselves. My own children have used some of the approaches in this book to deal with criticism, teasing, ridicule, coercion, and conflict.

These skills are a kind of verbal judo—a term that has been used by others, most prominently George Thompson, to refer to verbal techniques that can help us deal with difficult social situations. Of all the schools of martial arts, judo is perhaps the most assertive without being overtly aggressive. The techniques of judo are relatively gentle in the sense that they are directed toward deflecting or controlling an attack. Students don't attempt to strike with punches, kicks, or other offensive moves but rather apply throwing and grappling moves in order to use an attacker's force to their own advantage. Similarly, verbal judo isn't meant to be used to lash out and attack others aggressively but rather to respond assertively to their verbal blows.

One of the strengths of martial arts training is that students learn very clear and specific techniques. With one little step at a time, they develop a repertoire of moves that they can ultimately use in any combination they need. My techniques work the same way. By practicing and mastering them one step at a time, your children can become better equipped to deal with difficult social situations as they arise in everyday living.

Kids have always faced these tough situations. But with the current pattern of family and work life, parents frequently aren't around to provide support (it's been estimated that as of 1986, parents had ten to twelve hours less time each week to spend with their children than in 1960). Children need to have skills to fend for themselves when we're not there. They also need the skills to deal with us, their own parents, especially when, too distracted by the daily hustle and bustle, we forget to be kind and reasonable.

WAKING UP TO OUR KIDS

My kids are amazed at my unique paternal ability to not hear them at times. They can be standing two feet in front of me, and if I'm absorbed in something else, I don't hear a thing they're saying. They ask their mother, "How can Dad do that?" as if it were a special power. Sometimes they're truly impressed by this ability and they take turns testing it out. But mostly they're annoyed. This worries me because I'm afraid at some point they'll give up and stop trying. I need to pay attention to my children if I want them to pay attention to me.

If our kids have become bothersome speed bumps, we need to wake up and pull off the road before we really hurt somebody.

The first step in successfully keeping our children is literally to *wake up* to them! If we've chosen to have children and then have allowed careers or other ambitions to replace them as a primary purpose in life, we need to wake up to the sobering fact that we've been fooled by the false prophets of our materialistic, Madison Avenue culture. If we've turned over to others the heavy lifting of training and mentoring our children, we need to pay much more attention to the content and approach of that training and become involved with it. More critically, if our kids have become bothersome speed bumps for us on a fast, furious, autopilot ride through life, we need to wake up and pull off the road before we really hurt somebody.

A 1997 study conducted by the University of Michigan's Institute for Social Research confirmed that committed parents make a difference. Even after accounting for those things that parents have little control over, the study concluded that parents who report being close to their children, having warm relationships with them, doing more things with them, and maintaining high expectations for them have children who seem happier, better behaved, and better adjusted socially.

We need to slow down and make time for our kids. By ceasing to judge them, and consciously returning our minds and hearts to our present moments with them, we can wake up to understand their unique natures and needs. We can wake up to think about what we can do to help them be happy and resilient human beings. We can wake up to treat them with patience, acceptance, and understanding, and not with impulsive outbursts of anger. We can wake up to turn off (or toss out) the TV and other distractions, and simply be with them to talk, listen, and play.

In their book *Reinventing Your Life,* the psychologists Jeffrey Young and Janet Klosko refer to six basic needs that must be met in order for our children to thrive:

1. Basic safety
2. Connection to others
3. Autonomy
4. Self-esteem
5. Self-expression
6. Realistic limits

Part of waking up to our parental opportunities and responsibilities is to wake up to these needs and determine how to help them be met. Being a successful parent is very difficult, but it's almost impossible if we're not consciously awake to it.

For most of us, learning to wake up and live consciously in the present moment takes some real effort. I strongly recommend the writings of both Jon Kabat-Zinn and Thich Nhat Hanh as guides to developing a personal practice of being really awake in our lives, a practice also known as mindfulness.

In no area of our lives is mindfulness more important than in the realm of living with and teaching our children. This is especially true when our children are still becoming fully formed human beings, when their internal toolboxes are waiting to be filled. In Chapter 7, I've included some practices that you can use to help both your children and you develop greater mindfulness in

> MINDFULNESS
>
> Mindfulness means paying attention in a particular way: on purpose, in the present moment, and nonjudgmentally. This kind of attention nurtures greater awareness, clarity and acceptance of present-moment reality. It wakes us up to the fact that our lives unfold only in moments. If we are not fully present for many of those moments, we may not only miss what is most valuable in our lives but also fail to realize the richness and the depth of our possibilities for growth and transformation.
>
> —JON KABAT-ZINN

everyday living. I've also included a reading list of helpful books that deal with the formal and informal practice of mindfulness.

HOW THIS VERBAL TOOLBOX SYSTEM WORKS

The system presented in this book is based on many of the common principles used in assertiveness training: self-expression, disclosure, deflection, verbal repetition, and problem/conflict resolution skills. I've tried to blend helpful adult techniques into this system in a form that is simple enough for children to understand. I've also included elements of cognitive therapy and mindfulness, which I believe are essential for developing lasting internal assertiveness and well-being.

The Verbal Toolbox is

- divided into seven categories I call Ways, each named for a different type of bird
- composed of basic, simple techniques or practices for each category
- introduced by brief, easy-to-use, parent scripts

I've chosen birds as the symbols for my verbal toolbox because of their unique vocal nature and because of my appreciation for their presence in the world. It wasn't always so for me. I had held a certain mental image of "birders" (as you probably do): goofy hats, knee-high socks, and librarian-type spectacles and binoculars dangling from their necks. So I found it particularly humorous that my two athletic brothers and nephew were so seriously involved in birding. But the weekend following my father's funeral, I was in the mood for Point Reyes, the Pacific Ocean, the healing balm of nature, and the company of my brothers and nephew. I was grateful for their invitation to join them and for what I experienced. I've enjoyed birding ever since.

It's instructive to note that while many birdcalls are innate (especially the short, generic alarm calls), many species learn the specific song elements of their repertoire from one or more adult tutors. Through vocal imitation, young songbirds learn the more elaborate structures of their dialect that are essential to survival and success within their species. I believe there's a good analogy here for us as humans. Our own young need conscious tutoring to learn the verbal and mental tools that they'll need to help them be happy and self-reliant within our world. We often assume that they'll simply pick up these skills. And often they will, from imitating our models and the models of others. But equally often they'll need conscious help in learning these skills—just as they need help in learning reading, math, ballet, or anything else.

I've named each of my seven Ways of verbal tools after a specific bird whose characteristics best describe it. Kids respond naturally to birds, and these images are easy to remember. Children as young as five can readily recall a chattering blue jay, darting hummingbird, or wise owl and the verbal skills associated with each.

Within each of the seven categories of verbal skills, I've included specific techniques. My experience tells me that it can be valuable to have a memorable name attached to a technique. The name becomes shorthand for reminding children of what they've been taught. When you refer to the Mighty Might or the Sherlock Holmes, your child will recognize the technique immediately.

You can introduce these verbal Ways systematically or on an as-needed basis. Pick out what is useful and toss the rest. If you want to provide a general overview of these principles, as I did, it may be constructive to have more formal introductory sessions on a periodic basis. You'll find a summary checklist at the back of the book to keep track of what your child has learned if you want a more systematic approach. The scripts are meant not to be used verbatim but to give you some ideas on how the logic of the introduction might flow.

COACHING TIPS

Having these verbal techniques at my quick disposal has helped my own parenting. As much as anything, they've provided my family with a way to talk about, and follow up on, important social and intrapersonal skills. When a teacher in school says, "Try using multiplication instead of division," or "Use the long *o* sound instead of the short *o* sound," children know exactly what the teacher is saying and can respond accordingly. When I tell players in a basketball scrimmage to pivot and block out, they understand what I'm saying. Likewise, when I tell my daughter to try the Power I or the Shrug, she knows exactly what I mean. I've included scripts and examples in language basic enough for kids ages five and above to understand. If your child is especially verbal, you might introduce the Ways even earlier. Of course, you'd tailor the level of language in the examples to your child's needs.

When I first began teaching these techniques, my kids were ten, seven, and four. I wanted to give them a general overview, so I would make one of the Ways a theme for the month. Each week I would briefly introduce a technique and review what we'd talked about the week before. We would do a lot of role playing. I found that it's especially important to do reverse role playing, where I play the child, so that my kids can see a model of how to use the technique. At the end of the month I would give them a symbol of the Way as a gift and memory (for example, a necklace, baseball hat, poster, or other trinket).

As with any training process, the introduction is usually the easy part. But I've also found that the ongoing coaching and review, if not easy, can at least be simple. The keys to coaching are clarity, timely pointers, and knowing your children. This book provides techniques, examples, and exercises to clarify the tools. Timely pointers means offering your kids a review of the tools in on-the-spot, real-life situations (not unlike stopping a scrimmage or calling a time-out in the middle of a game, to point some things out). Knowing your children means staying close to them and understanding their needs. To be effective I believe that all mentoring and coaching of our children needs to be done as naturally and unobtrusively as possible.

Here are some examples of how I've integrated coaching these tools into the natural flow of my own life:

- When my children come to me and begin blaming each other for some incident or infraction, I ask them to go back and use direct communication with each other first (the Power I, see p. 22), and if that doesn't work we have a Solution Time (see Chapter 4).
- When teasing or bickering gets out of control, I require Kind Talk (Chapter 5), and I sit down with the one who's being teased and review the tools for responding to teasing (the Way of the Hummingbird). I use the Power I myself to tell my kids what I want.
- If I'm legitimately correcting my kids and they start to get abnormally defensive, I refer them to the tools for dealing constructively with criticism (the Way of the Crow).
- If my kids are struggling with a task that they really need to finish, I sit down and help them with the But Twist (Chapter 6) or refer them to what practicing the Rock (Chapter 7) was like and how it might apply.
- When I notice over time, either from direct observation or from what they tell me about school, that my kids can benefit by using a specific technique, I go back and review it with them.

I don't make a big deal out of it, and I don't constantly "technique" my children. But I do have the tools I can casually refer to when I need to and when I feel it's a good time to interject some suggestions. A key tip is to use a lot of Solution Time at first—a time-out from difficult situations and a time-in to help your kids solve difficulties creatively and reinforce verbal tools. After a certain point, my children became so tired of me calling for a Solution Time that they began masterfully to solve more of their interpersonal problems on their own.

You clearly have to be very patient and not too pushy, especially with very young children. My youngest child (daughter, Brooke) was a preschooler when I began to teach my children (she would refer to our verbal judo as "purple" judo, a phrase we still love to use). At this stage of life, feelings can be so overwhelming that it's hard for kids to use anything but a verbal hammer when they get frustrated or afraid. They mostly just need our love, patience, and support. But it wasn't too early for Brooke at least to begin to understand the concepts and become familiar with the language. It also wasn't too early for her to have a Solution Time with her big brothers to try to solve their problems together.

On the other end of the scale, the bird analogies might not appeal to teenagers, and teens might not like a structure that's too formal. My oldest son, Adam, is now a teenager, and he clearly doesn't like a lot of lengthy talk. However, teenagers are still teachable if we're more casual about it and not too preachy. With teenagers we need to find our spots for informal coaching. I've found them to be open to tips and even to fun role playing.

My middle son, Jackson, is now at a prime age, eleven, for coaching. He's old enough to understand things clearly and is open to training from his parents. This is the stage to really fill the toolbox, so that when our children aren't as open to our coaching, they've already learned the tools and beliefs that can be of help to them independently.

Over time some of these tools and practices have become a part of my children's verbal toolboxes. They've gradually become a part of our family language and culture. This isn't to say that my children don't have the same tumult and bad moments that all children have. But it does mean that they have fewer of them, they deal with them better, and I know what to tell them when they need help. Using these practices has also given me a forum for discussing with my children certain beliefs that I think will help them to be happy and to do good.

We have only a few, brief years to enjoy and influence our children. I believe that the greatest influence we can have on our children, beyond just loving them and staying close to them, is to teach them principles (by both word and deed) that can help them to be happy and to do good. These verbal techniques and practices have assisted me in that pursuit.

A WORD OF CAUTION

How we train is as important as what we train. It can't be overemphasized how important it is to train with love and patience. We're only trying to give our children some tools; we're not trying to create perfectly assertive children or to achieve perfection as trainer-parents.

We've all witnessed Little League coaches who are seriously preparing themselves for the Major Leagues and it isn't pretty. The best Little League coaches are those who teach a few pointers, play catch with the kids, encourage them, and then let them play. They understand that their goal is the development and well-being of the kids, not the final winning score. So it is with teaching our children these verbal skills. We need to show children how to use the techniques (the pointers), do some fun role playing together (playing catch), encourage them, and then simply let them have at it. It's particularly important not to get down on them if they don't use techniques correctly or at all in real life. The whole idea is to provide our kids with some tools, not to impose on them another set of performance standards.

The best Little League coaches understand that their goal is the development and well-being of the kids, not the final winning score. So it is with teaching our children these verbal skills.

Finally, we need to be careful about our core beliefs about "our" children. If taken too literally, this "our" concept can make us think of children as possessions rather than independent humans. We're blessed to have our children come through us, but they are not us. They need our leadership, guidance, and love, but not our control. We have to let them blossom into their own uniqueness. Our once-in-a-lifetime privilege and calling as parents is to help nurture this blossoming for another human being.

CHAPTER ONE

The Way of the Blue Jay: Assertive Self-expression

Spend a little time in the forest, and you quickly learn that the blue jay is exceptionally expressive. You may not see its beautiful blue wings and crown as it darts from tree to tree, but you'll always be able to hear its squawking, no matter where you are. The blue jay will be continuously and fearlessly telling you and all its other neighbors how it feels about things. The Way of the Blue Jay is the way of assertive self-expression, or telling others how you feel.

Several years ago I taught and coached a Spanish-speaking migrant student named Gonzalo. Despite the fact that he was as economically poor as poor can get, Gonzalo believed that he was just as good as anybody else in the high school (he was actually better than about anybody else when it came to running track). His naturally assertive way was sometimes misinterpreted by English-speaking students, and I would find myself keeping him out of skirmishes. Gonzalo had an innate sense of a noble birthright that transcended economic status or any other circumstance.

Some kids, like Gonzalo, are naturally assertive from the moment they're born. If your child is one of these naturally assertive people, this chapter will be overkill. Your challenge is probably to teach your child kindness and respectfulness. But many children, because of either their innate personalities or the way they've been influenced by parents and others, have a difficult time dealing assertively with people who are being bothersome. If they've developed a fear of having people get angry with them, or a fear of disapproval or ridicule, they probably won't stand up for themselves. By contrast, if they've developed a belief that their self-worth is based on always being right and not making mistakes (perfectionism), they may aggressively "lash out"—in order to protect their "selves."

Children with these traits can't deal completely comfortably with difficult social exchanges until they've internalized new beliefs about themselves. As long as they don't have a core belief that they're fundamentally good, no matter what people think of them or say to them, they'll likely be inclined to be "walked over" or to lash out in confrontational situations. Either they won't express themselves, out of fear of anger or ridicule, or they'll repeatedly try to roll right over people, in an effort to be right at all costs and preserve their egos.

The middle ground between these two responses is assertiveness: a clear expression of our interests, feelings, and opinions, without intent to roll over others. Again, comfortable assertiveness springs from a healthy core assumption: Your children believe that they're just as good as anybody else.

Until your children have developed and internalized this core belief with your active and conscious help, practicing the verbal techniques of the Way of the Blue Jay can help them deal with social situations where assertiveness would be beneficial. And who better to practice these techniques with than you? For better or worse, parents often represent imposing authority figures in their children's lives.

Assertiveness: a clear expression of our interests, feelings, and opinions, without intent to roll over others.

SCRIPT TO INTRODUCE THE WAY OF THE BLUE JAY

If you go and sit quietly in many forests, you'll often hear a loud squawking sound from a certain bird. It's usually the sound of the blue jay. If you're lucky enough to see a blue jay, you'll see that it's constantly jabbering away at its fellow creatures in the forest and telling them how it feels about things.

Blue jays are good examples of assertive self-expression—which means telling people exactly what you want and how you feel about things. Sometimes in life people may be unkind, they may try to get you to do things you don't really want to do, or they may try to keep you from getting things that you deserve. When people are bothering you, the first thing to do is simply to tell them to stop. We can never be sure that others understand how we feel until we tell them. Telling them how we feel may not solve the problem, but it's the best place to start.

The Way of the Blue Jay is learning to tell people directly how we feel about things.

Technique 1: Power I

The Power I, not to be confused with the famous football formation, is a technique that's meant to help your children get into the habit of assertively expressing what they want or what they feel by using "I" statements—as in "I want," "I don't want," "I like," "I don't like," "I feel," "I think," "I am," "I disagree." It's a way of helping your kids regain their sense of sovereignty if they've lost it. It may seem obvious that kids naturally know how to do this. As very small children they certainly know how to cry out for what they want in a very uninhibited way—in fact, there are times when we wish they were a tad more inhibited. But as they develop, sometimes people get angry at them when they express their feelings and ask for what they want; they learn that it is "selfish"—and therefore they're bad—to ask for what they want; or they may find it easier to get what they want by indirect means. They learn that it's not okay to disagree. With no other outlet for honest, direct communication, kids can become very astute at getting what they want indirectly—through playing the role of the victim and using the tools of blame, exaggeration, and manipulation. The Power I is meant to help them get more comfortable in using direct communication.

The Power I is simply using the word "I" in a clear, confident manner to express desires and feelings in confrontational situations: "I want you to stop doing that," "I feel bad when you do that," "I want you to leave me alone," "I want you to stop teasing me," "I feel like you're not listening," "I want you to help me clean up," "I disagree with that," "I don't like that," "I feel angry when you say that," and so on. The important thing is for children to get in the habit of feeling comfortable about simply and directly expressing what they want and don't want, and how they feel and think, in a variety of situations with friends, foes, and authority figures alike. They need to learn that there is no need to blame others—since that only tends to create additional conflict.

I try to praise my children on the spot if they use the Power I with me in situations where I'm being unfair or unkind. Not only is it valuable for me to be reminded in those situations, but these moments are very valuable for my children. If they can deal directly with me in those situations, I'm more confident they'll be able to deal effectively with other authority figures later in their lives. They also need to understand that adults aren't always right or reasonable and that it's okay to disagree with them so long as it's done respectfully. Sometimes as parents we get insecure about our authority and about always needing to be right. We sometimes see ourselves as the rulers of our homes, as opposed to the leaders of our homes. If you ever have doubts about the benefits of an authoritarian parenting style versus a more democratic one, just remember that studies of Nazi Germany generally conclude that autocratic, authoritarian family systems helped to make the outcomes of that society possible. People listen to and follow leaders; they either submit to or fight dictators. As parents we need to be assertive in our own right with our children. We need to maintain expectations, rules, and consequences. But we also need to avoid being autocratic.

If my children's use of the Power I is unreasonable, I simply give them a Power I right back (the Power I technique is as important for parents to use as it is for children). I don't yield my parental leadership role in the family, but back-and-forth verbal interchange is very healthy in helping our children get a sense of sovereignty in their lives. Using the Power I in an uninhibited, direct way can be the beginning of a more happy life.

Script to Introduce the Power I

The Power I is the first step of the Way of the Blue Jay. It's the best way to get people to understand what you want and how you feel about things. We sometimes think that people should automatically know how we feel about things. But unless we tell them, we can't *really* be sure that they understand. We need to tell others if they're bothering us or if we don't like something. We need to tell them how we want to be treated.

The Power I is simply using the word "I"—as in "I want you to stop doing that," "I want you to leave me alone," "I feel bad when you do that," "I don't want you to do that," "I feel angry when you say that," "I disagree with that," "I feel like you're not listening to me," "I want you to help me clean up," and so on. It's getting comfortable using the word "I" to tell others what you want or how you feel. You can also use the Power I to tell people that you don't agree with them, that you have different opinions than they do. We don't need to blame people by using the "you" word, we can just tell them how we feel by using the "I" word.

You need to know that in our home, I want you to feel like you can use the Power I anytime, because I really want to know how you honestly feel about things. You need to feel like you can come to me at any time with your feelings and problems. You also need to use the Power I on me when I do or say things that bother you or make you feel bad, or when I say things that you disagree with.

The best way to learn the Power I is through practicing it together. So I'm going to give you some situations, and I want you to use the Power I on me. Sometimes it's especially hard to use the Power I on your friends, other kids your age, or adults who are in charge, like your teacher. So later on I'm going to give you some tips on how you can say things to them if it's kind of hard.

Practicing the Power I Together:

Role-Playing Examples

Feel free to substitute your own age-relevant wording.

Parent: Let's say I come up to you and start calling you names.

Child: I want you to stop doing that.

Parent: Let's say someone is playing with a special toy (game) and you don't want them playing with it.

Child: I don't want you to play with that toy.

Parent: Let's say I come home cranky from work and in a very mean voice I yell at you to get in there and clean up your room.

Child: I'll clean up my room, but I don't like it when you talk to me so mean.

Parent: Let's say a kid at school butts in and starts using the computer even though you've been waiting for it for a long time.

Child: I was here first; it's actually my turn.

Parent: Let's say you're with a group of kids at school and it's time to clean up but they're not helping you.

Child: Hey, I want you guys to help me clean up.

Parent: Let's say you're trying to tell me something that's very important to you and I just keep reading my newspaper, not paying attention to you.

Child: I have something to tell you, and I feel bad when you don't listen. I really want you to listen.

Parent: For other kids or adults who make it uncomfortable for you to use the Power I, here are some ways to say things that might make it easier.

This may sound dumb, but I don't like that.

This is hard for me to tell you, but I don't like that.

I hope you won't feel bad, but I don't agree.

You may not like to hear this, but I don't like that.

You'll probably get mad, but I don't like that.

Not to sound mean or anything, but I don't agree.

You may disagree, but I don't like that.

Call me crazy, but I don't agree.

Listen, bub, you may not like it, but I don't like that.

Parent: The important thing isn't how you get to the Power I but that you do get there, and that you actually tell others how you feel. Sometimes you might feel very nervous about using the Power I. This is normal. But remember that you can always still say the words—and it doesn't matter how you say the words or how nervous you sound. Just say them when you need to. Are there any kinds of situations that make it hard for you to tell people how you really feel? Okay, let's practice those situations together.

Technique 2: No Thanks

As parents we know that our children actually know "no" very well. Next to "why?" it's one of the first words they latch on to. They may not understand the meaning of the word when we use it, but they clearly understand it when they use it. In most families kids are very uninhibited in their use of "no" with parents and siblings (at least when they're out of earshot of others). Unfortunately, as they grow up, they sometimes have real problems using both "no" and "why?" with other people when they need to. A desire for acceptance overcomes their desire for independence (at least from peers).

Like the Power I, No Thanks is a very simple technique of verbal assertiveness. If children don't learn to feel comfortable in saying no, without need for explanation, to any person in any situation, they risk the likelihood of moments of extreme unhappiness in their lives. Our lives become greatly defined by what things we say no to, as well as what things we say yes to.

It's one thing to say yes to things that we truly want to do and feel right about; it's quite another to say yes out of habit or out of fear (again because of core beliefs relating to self-worth). In particular, adolescents, fearful of ridicule, disapproval, and isolation, find it difficult to say no thanks comfortably. The things they say yes to can change the course of their entire lives for better or for worse.

According to statistics published by the U.S. Department of Health and Human Services in 1998, in some important areas children haven't learned to say no very well at all. Use of illicit drugs in a given month by twelfth-graders had increased by 60 percent between 1991 and 1997, and cigarette smoking by high schoolers had risen by 25 percent during the same period. Although modestly leveling off in the 1990s, violent crime arrest rates for seventeen-year-olds had increased by 138 percent between 1980 and 1996. Participation in binge drinking (31 percent of twelfth-graders in 1996), being in a car with a driver who's driving under the influence of alcohol (42 percent of high schoolers in a given month, as of 1995), and teenage experience with sex (66 percent of high school seniors, as of 1995) have all reached alarming levels. Our children need to be taught from an early age to provide an assertive "no thanks" when they need to.

As hard as it is, if I want my children to have the independence to tell peers and others no, I've got to be open-minded in allowing them to tell me no. I can't beat them up verbally when they say they don't want to do something and expect that it'll be easy for them to say no assertively to others. I've got to discern patiently and wisely whether their no is reasonable or not. If their no is unreasonable, then I can simply require that they do what I'm asking anyway. If their no is belligerent and disrespectful, I need to assertively tell them how I want to be treated. But, within reason, they need to have the emotional room to be able at least to tell me no.

Script to Introduce No Thanks

No Thanks is the second technique of the Way of the Blue Jay. This technique is used in situations where people ask us to do things we don't want to do or we know aren't good for us to do. In life, a lot of our happiness is based on the things we say no to. Sometimes it's just a matter of saying no to things that we don't like or enjoy. Other times it's even more important, because it's saying no to things that can do harm to ourselves or others [give your children examples of some of these harmful things].

Just like with the Power I, I want you to feel free to tell me when you don't want to do things. I may disagree, and you may have to do them anyway. Remember that I want you to speak to me respectfully. But I still want to know how you feel about things and why you feel the way you do.

It was hard sometimes for me when I was a kid to say no to my friends, and it might be hard for you. But just like the Power I, it's not how you get there but that you do ultimately get there and say no when you need to.

There are a bunch of ways to say no comfortably; here are some examples.

NO

No, but thanks for asking.

No, but thanks for thinking of me.

No, but maybe another time.

No, I guess I'm just a chicken.

No way, let's do something else.

No, but it sounds like a lot of fun—my loss.

No, I just can't.

No, I won't be able to.

No, I'm just not comfortable with that.

No, this is probably dumb, but I just don't want to.

No, I know I should, but I'm just going to pass.

No, my parents would kill me.

No, I just don't want to.

No way, José.

No, take a hike.

No, no, a thousand times no.

The best way to learn the No Thanks is for us to practice together. I'll give you some situations, and you use a No Thanks on me.

Practicing No Thanks Together:

Role-Playing Examples

Feel free to substitute your own age-relevant wording.

Parent: Let's say I'm one of your friends, and I say, "Hey, let's go over and push that little kid around."

Child: No way.

Parent: Let's say you're over at a friend's house, and he says, "Hey, my parents aren't around, let's watch this cool R-rated movie."

Child: No thanks; let's go out and shoot hoops.

Parent: Let's say someone invites you to play or go to a party, but you don't want to go.

Child: No, but thanks for inviting me.

Parent: Let's say someone passes a bottle of beer over to you and says, "Hey, have a swig or two."

Child: No way, José.

Parent: Let's say we've told you that you need to come home from your friend's house by a certain time, and your friend says, "You don't need to go home, just stay for another half hour or so."

Child: No, I'd really like to but I can't.

Parent: Let's say a teacher at school asks you to join a club that you don't really want to join.

Child: No, but thanks for asking.

Parent: Is it ever hard for you to say no in certain situations or with certain types of people? What kinds of situations or people? Okay, let's practice those situations together.

Technique 3: Simple Questions

Most of us have been in a class, meeting, or other situation when we suddenly realize that we don't have a clue what the speaker has just been saying. Either we weren't paying attention or we didn't understand. Sometimes we're too embarrassed to say anything, and we sit there in ignorance. It's always a great relief when one of those unkempt, back-row types asks all the "dumb" questions that the rest of us are too afraid to ask.

As humans we need to come to grips with our reality: We're not perfect. We don't know all things, we don't understand all things, we don't always pay attention, and we sometimes get bored. And sometimes people don't explain things very well. This is part of our existence, yet we've convinced ourselves otherwise. We can and should ask as many questions as we need to until we understand. Newspaper reporters implement this technique very well, and so can the rest of us.

There's nothing more assertive than asking simple questions until we get answers that we need. With the Power I we *tell* people what we want; with Simple Questions we *ask* people for what we want (usually information). Theodore Levitt, a former professor at the Harvard Business School, has suggested that one of the most important qualities of effective business leaders is their willingness to ask simple questions: Why do we do it? Why that way? How much does it cost? Who does it cheaper and better? and so on. What works for business in this case works for everything else in life. As individuals, families, companies, and nations, we waste great amounts of time, energy, money, and even lives by not just asking simple questions. We have a natural tendency to react and to do before we ask and get answers. Only when we get clear answers to simple questions can we make reasonable choices.

Most children, when they're very young, are great at asking questions. They can wear us out with their questioning. But as with telling others what they want (Power I) or saying no (No Thanks), children sometimes have this natural inclination driven out of them. They're sometimes taught that it's not polite to ask too many questions, that they don't need to know certain things, that parents and others don't have much patience with questions. Sometimes they receive ridicule and laughter when they ask questions. By the time they're older, surrounded by peer influences, they're hypervigilant about appearances. They don't want to ever appear dumb in front of their peers or teachers by asking simple questions that might be perceived as ignorant.

Mastering simple questions means giving ourselves license just to keep asking all the simple questions we need to until we get answers. Simple questions like why? why not? why would that be true? what if? what is that? how does it work? how do you know that? what does that mean? help us get to the crux of an issue. Larry King maintains that the greatest simple question of all is why? Why? is great because it forces people to explain things. If people can't answer why? in ways that make sense, we know that they may not know what they're talking about. Richard Feynman, one of the world's leading physicists, maintained that we should always be suspicious of ideas that can't be simply explained. He believed that most experts don't know more than the average person. Anybody can produce a study to support his or her ideas. For Feynman, the important simple question was How did they find that out?

We can greatly help our children by creating an environment where they feel that it's okay to ask lots of simple questions. We do them no favors when we ask their questions for them. We can give them moral support by being with them when they need to ask questions over the telephone, in stores, and other places, but they need to ask simple questions themselves. We need to help our children to just keep asking.

Script to Introduce Simple Questions

The third technique of the Way of the Blue Jay is called Simple Questions. Many times in life we need to get information. We need to get information to do schoolwork, to find things, to buy things, to get help, to make choices, and to figure out if others are telling us the truth. The best first step in getting information is just to ask lots of questions. Asking questions saves a lot of time when you're trying to get information. Since you're as good as anybody else, you can feel free to ask questions of anyone—both kids and adults. With the Power I you learned to *tell* others what you want. With Simple Questions you *ask* people for what you want. People don't know how you feel until you *tell* them, and they don't know what you want until you *ask* them. It doesn't matter at all if you're nervous about asking questions or if your voice is a little shaky—the only thing that matters is that you ask simple questions when you need to.

The smartest thing in the world is to ask questions if we don't understand. Simple questions are never dumb. One of the very best simple questions is "why?" Ask why whenever you want people to explain things better or give you proof for something. You never have to agree with other people, and "why?" helps us to know if it makes sense to agree with people. Other good simple questions are "Why not?" "Why would that be true?" "What do you mean?" "How do you know that?" "How do you do this?" "How does this work?" "Could you explain that again?"

You always need to feel like you can ask any questions that you want to in our home. You always need to feel free to ask questions at school, in stores, or any other place. Just keep asking questions until you understand. This is a free country, and you're free just to keep asking. If it's hard for you to ask simple questions when you're in a big group, like a school class, make sure to go up afterward to the teacher or whoever was talking and ask the simple questions.

Let's practice Simple Questions. I'm going to give you some situations, and I want you to come up with some simple questions. Remember, Simple Questions means just asking all the simple questions you need to until you really understand.

Practicing Simple Questions Together:

Role-Playing Examples

Feel free to substitute your own age-relevant wording.

Parent: Let's say a teacher at school explains something and you don't really understand; what simple question could you ask?

Child: "Could you please explain that again?"

Parent: Let's say you're in the library and you need to find some information for homework, but you're a little embarrassed to ask the librarian; what simple question could you ask?

Child: "I'm doing a report and I need to find some information. Could you please help me?"

Parent: Let's say you're in a superfancy restaurant and you need to use the bathroom; what simple question could you ask?

Child: "Could you please tell me where the bathroom is?"

Parent: Let's say another kid comes up to you in class and says that he's in charge of cleanup and you need to clean up half the room all by yourself; what simple questions could you ask?

Child: "How come others aren't helping me?" or "Why did you decide it that way?" or "Who put you in charge?"

Parent: Let's say a substitute teacher at school makes a strange statement that you don't really believe, like "Class, remember that almost all people from Australia are really unfriendly"; what simple questions could you ask?

Child: "Why would that be true?" or "How do you know that's true?"

Parent: Let's say you're having a lot of fun at recess and one of your friends says, "You need to act more serious, you're acting too babyish for your age"; what simple questions could you ask?

Child: "Why?" or "Why does that matter to you?" or "Who said?"

Parent: Is it ever hard for you to ask questions in certain situations or with certain types of people? What kinds of situations or people? Okay, let's practice those situations together.

In everyday life, help your children think up simple questions and give them the moral support to ask them. Encourage them to ask you questions, including the "why?" question. If you feel that your older kids are asking questions in a way that's disrespectful, just tell them so.

For their general social development, have them make some of the routine telephone inquiries on behalf of the family. These can include calls to the store, the library, the movie theater, the information operator, and other places.

Technique 4: Squeaky Wheel

The squeaky wheel gets the oil (or was that the early bird gets the worm?). Which means that persistence pays. Sometimes the only difference between successful and unsuccessful assertiveness is a little persistence. Children need to understand that many times in their lives as they express what they want or don't want, people may simply try to disregard what they're saying, or they may use ridicule or anger or some other manipulative verbal method to try to get the children to change their minds or go away.

You want to give your children the tools to be able to deal verbally with people in difficult, emotionally charged situations—especially when people would like them simply to go away. Once again, children need to understand very clearly that they're as important and valuable as anyone else on the planet—including their friends, their teachers, the cashiers at the store, the star athletes at school, their parents, the president of the United States. They're as good as anybody else (but no better).

Developing this sense will help your children realize that they need not be intimidated by anyone in verbal situations—that they can express themselves and be persistent with anyone. At the same time, all children need to be taught to assess situations wisely and to avoid and disappear from situations with potentially dangerous people (note the Disappearing Act, in Chapter 3).

We're all familiar with the squeaky wheel analogy of persistence. The squeaky wheel is the one on a bicycle that gets the oil. In its best form, it's calmly repeating what you want or don't want until you get a reasonable response. Its defining quality is not giving in.

In the context of the Way of the Blue Jay, the Squeaky Wheel means giving your child the discipline to keep repeating the technique that's being used until the other person really hears what your child is saying and responds to it in a reasonable way. Without the Squeaky Wheel, techniques like Power I and No Thanks may prove ineffective. Some people need to understand clearly that children mean what they say before they will either accept or respond to their expressed wishes. The Squeaky Wheel is a tool that children can learn to develop verbal persistence.

Script to Introduce the Squeaky Wheel

I want you to remember that one of the most important things about the Way of the Blue Jay is persistence—which means not giving up. Persistence means just repeating yourself over and over, until people understand that you're not going to give up.

This technique is called the Squeaky Wheel because the squeaky wheel on a bicycle is the one that people pay attention to and finally put some oil on. In real life, adults and other kids may keep bugging you when you don't want them to, or they may keep pushing you to do things you don't want to do. They may think that if they make fun of you or keep pushing, you'll give up. All you've got to do is to keep trying more than they do. You've got to be like the squeaky wheel on the bicycle.

The Squeaky Wheel can be used with any of the other verbal techniques that you're learning. It means that you just keep squeaking—that you just keep on repeating the technique until you get the right response from the other person. If the person is doing something that could be harmful to you or someone else, don't be afraid to speak loudly or even yell until he or she gets the point. We're going to practice the Squeaky Wheel together first with the Power I and the No Thanks, but you should use it in the future with any of the other techniques. I'm going to give you some situations, and no matter what I say, I want you not to give up but just keep repeating either the Power I or the No Thanks.

You need to remember that if you're talking to very mean or dangerous people who might want to hurt you, don't use the Squeaky Wheel or say anything else, just leave quickly. This is called the Disappearing Act, and we'll talk about it later.

Practicing the Squeaky Wheel Together:

Role-Playing Examples

Feel free to substitute your own age-relevant wording.

Parent: Let's say I'm trying to get you to go to a party that you really don't want to go to, and I'm saying, "Come on, let's just go for a little while."

Child: No, but thanks anyway.

Parent: Come on, it'll be a lot of fun.

Child: No, I really don't feel like it.

Parent: Everyone will think you're stupid if you don't come.

Child: You might be right, but I just don't want to go.

Parent: You know, I go with you to stuff all the time.

Child: Yeah, you're right, but I still don't want to go.

Parent: Let's say one of your friends starts going through your refrigerator at home and you don't like it; pretend I'm your friend.

Child: This may sound dumb, but I don't like you looking through my refrigerator.

Parent: In just a second. I'm checking stuff out.

Child: No, I'm serious. I really don't like you doing that.

Parent: Give me a break—what's the big deal?

Child: It might be weird, but I just don't like it.

Parent: Let's say an older kid comes over during recess and says, "Listen, kid, you're a goof-off, why don't you act your age?"

Child: I don't want you to speak to me like that.

Parent: Listen, I'm older than you, I'll speak to you any way I want to.

Child: I still don't want you to say that.

Parent: Kids like you need to learn some respect.

Child: You might be right, but I still don't want you to speak to me like that.

Parent: Let's say an adult at a cash register hasn't given you the correct change.

Child: I'm sorry, but you didn't give me the correct change.

Parent: Sure I did, kid, I gave you two dollars.

Child: No, you only gave me one.

Parent: Listen, kid, I'm sure I gave you two.

Child: No, you only gave me one.

Parent: Hey, kid, you're holding up the line.

Child: I'm sorry, but you didn't give me the correct change.

Parent: Let's say a friend comes by, and you don't really want to play, but your friend asks, "Can you play?"

Child: I don't really want to play right now, but maybe tomorrow.

Parent: Why?

Child: I just don't want to.

Parent: Why?

Child: Just because.

Parent: But how come?

Child: Just because I don't want to today.

CHAPTER TWO

The Way of the Crow: Responding to Blame

Crows and blue jays come from the same family of very assertive birds. Ornithologists consider crows among the most intelligent species of birds. Farmers of the nineteenth century learned of their intelligence when they blamed crows for crop damage and attempted to eliminate them. Not only did crows survive but today they're one of the most abundant bird species on the planet. The Way of the Crow is the way of intelligently and calmly responding to blame.

Comedians often point to death and taxes as the two things in life that we can count on. They could easily add blame to that list. In our current litigious, politically correct culture, blame has taken on unhealthy proportions. We *blame* the Puritans for this tendency in our society, but let's be honest, the Puritans were just a tiny group of religious separatists who were briefly established in America about four hundred years ago. The fact that we even blame our blaming on somebody else (especially dead somebody elses) has a wry humor all its own.

Unfortunately, we're continuously flooded by the media, schools, religious institutions, special-interest groups (on both sides of the political spectrum), social critics, and government officials with the belief that if people think a certain way, say the wrong words, do something imperfectly, or make a mistake, they aren't good. We live in an era of social perfectionism. It's very natural for a child to fear blame in such an unyielding environment. Blame is particularly intimidating because children can easily conclude that if they *do* something bad, they in fact *are* bad. And if a culture has an enormous list of what's "bad" (everything from not wearing the right clothes or being thin enough to not being in step with popular modes of belief or lifestyle), the reasons for being bad can be overwhelming. The irony is that this is happening at a time when behavioral mores are actually "looser" than they've been in the past.

As parents we basically want two things for our children: We want them to be happy and do good. The biggest influence on their happiness is what they believe about themselves. The optimal belief we can give our kids about themselves is that they are fundamentally good—no matter what. The optimal belief that we can give them about doing good is that doing good is always right—no matter what. But if we carelessly mix these two beliefs, for example, by insisting that our children *are* good only when they *do* good, we set them up for a lifetime of turbulence and insecurity. Even when they do good, they may be doing it not for the simple sake of doing the good that needs to be done—but rather for the sake of being able to feel good inside.

It's vital that we teach our children clear rules of right and wrong. But we ought to keep our core moral code as short as possible, not as long as possible.

Make no mistake about it, it's vital that we teach our children clear rules of right and wrong, and that we maintain high expectations with respect to those rules. But we ought to keep our core moral code as short as possible, not as long as possible. As an example, the Ten Commandments remain, through the ages, a wonderful "short list" of serious baseline moral expectations. An even more condensed version is the "Golden Rule" taught by Jesus and others: to treat others as we would want to be treated. But beyond situations that require a response from our core moral code, there are the many other activities in life—all subject to plenty of human error, mistakes, and accidents. There's no good reason for our children to be emotionally imprisoned by a list that is too long and broad—whether that list comes from us or from society at large. We need to counter unnecessary expectations placed on our children by the surrounding society.

It's also clearly important for children to feel regret when they intentionally do harm. Regret can lead to recognition (waking up) and change. But there's a big difference between feeling temporary regret (guilt) over a harmful act and feeling self-loathing (shame) over natural, human, everyday mistakes or accidents. Some things just happen. It's part of the inherent nature of humankind to do and to try—and the results of that doing and trying have nothing to do with the inherent worth of people. Certainly there are a small percentage of people who, despite their initial worth as creations, have developed very harmful and dangerous natures. There are people whose characters have become seriously flawed and harmful. Children need to learn to protect themselves and others from such people, just as they would protect themselves from dangers in nature. But that leaves the rest of humanity—including themselves: worthwhile human beings who try natural things, make natural mistakes, and have natural strengths and weaknesses.

Our children need to accept themselves as effortlessly and readily as they would the ocean, the stars, and the mountains. We're even more amazing creations.

It would be reasonable for us to ask ourselves if a river or a cliff was dangerous or not, but it would seem absurd for us to ask if a river or a cliff was bad or not. Yet too many humans, who aren't even remotely harmful or dangerous, readily ruminate over what they perceive as their defectiveness and badness. We're at least as good as any other creation on the planet. Children need to accept themselves as effortlessly and readily as they would the ocean, the stars, and the mountains. When we deeply observe the amazing structure and systems that make up our minds and bodies and notice the internal wonder of our spiritual nature, we can see that we're even more amazing than these other creations.

Children also need to understand that they're not their thoughts. This may seem obvious, but it usually isn't. If someone expresses criticism of them, the thought may enter their minds that they not only screwed up but are screwups. Children need to be taught that no matter the source of such thoughts—others or themselves—those thoughts can never be them. They simply are. A thought about a mountain is not the mountain and cannot change it in any way—it's just a thought. Similarly, thoughts about our children are not our children, they're just thoughts.

Finally, we need to be particularly wise in how we correct our children. Our natural tendency as parents is to criticize too much (and express appreciation too little). We ought to save our corrections for when they really matter. The best way to correct is the way we've already learned—to simply and clearly use the Power I. We need to tell our kids what we want and how we feel; we don't need to blame them, ask them guilt-inducing questions, or say things that make them believe they're fundamentally not good. I've found it helpful to take my children aside separately and sit down next to them when I correct them. This way I don't embarrass them in front of others and it's also harder for me to speak in mean, angry tones when I'm right next to them.

> CORRECTING OUR CHILDREN
>
> Do: Use the Power I: "I want you to . . . ," "I don't want you to . . . ," "I feel bad when . . . ," "Please don't . . . ," and so on.
>
> Don't: Use blame or guilt-inducing "you" or "should" statements and questions: "You should really know better," "How could you . . .?" "Why did you . . .?" "What is your problem?" "Can't you do anything right?" and so on.

On those occasions when we do need to be firm and forceful, better to tell them what we want with a few sharp words (using the Power I) than to go on and on with guilt-inducing nagging.

The techniques of the Way of the Crow are meant to give children the tools to respond to blame in our contemporary world of heightened criticism.

SCRIPT TO INTRODUCE THE WAY OF THE CROW

Crows are among the smartest types of birds. Many years ago farmers blamed crows for eating their crops, and they tried to get rid of all the crows. But the crows were able to outsmart the farmers. Today crows are one of the most abundant types of birds on the earth. If you've seen crows in flight, maybe you've noticed how when they're bothered by much smaller birds they just continue on their way, not even troubled. The way crows have intelligently and calmly responded to blame is a good example for us. The Way of the Crow is the way of responding to blame from others.

In our family we have a very important moral code—which means we have a list of serious rules of right and wrong that we believe in and expect you to live by. [This is a good time to review your "short list" serious moral code with your children—where it comes from, why you believe in it, and why you expect them to keep it.] But many everyday mistakes and accidents occur to all of us. Sometimes we get blamed for our mistakes and accidents. One thing you've got to always remember is that it's normal and natural for people to make mistakes and have accidents. Nobody's perfect. It's good to feel bad if you've done things that have harmed others, and it's good to apologize and make up for those things. We expect you to learn from harmful mistakes and not to make them again. We don't want you to do bad things. But it's not good to feel that you're bad if you make mistakes. That's like saying that a deer is bad because it trips in the forest, or that a fish is bad because it swims in the wrong direction. So if you ever have feelings that you're a bad person because of mistakes or accidents, or for any other reason, you and I need to talk about it. Remember that we always love you no matter what.

We've already learned a technique that you can use in dealing with blame—the Power I. The Power I is always the best place to start when something is bothering you. You can always just tell people what you don't like.

The Way of the Crow introduces three new techniques that you can use when you're blamed. These can be used by themselves or along with the Power I.

Technique 5: Mea Culpa

Just make a mild suggestion to your teenager that he or she needs to spend less time on the telephone, and you'll find out how sensitive kids can be to criticism. Some kids can feel such a connection between blame and self-regard that within supersonic speed they get defensive over any criticism at all—even when it's accurate. And sometimes they clearly need some corrective criticism to help them get going in a different direction. Children may indeed not have done the chores they were supposed to do, they may get up late almost every day, they may have to stop teasing others, they may need to keep their rooms cleaner, and so forth.

When we or others point out their mistakes and undesirable actions, our children need a tool that can help them deal constructively with such correction. Having a handy tool can help reduce their fear of correction. Fear of criticism isn't healthy for either children or adults.

The Mea Culpa is a tool children can use when they're corrected or criticized and the facts of the criticism are mostly true. In essence, the Mea Culpa is applied by agreeing with the criticism or correction and providing sincere apologies. Out of fear or defensiveness, children in such situations sometimes spend a great deal of time trying to justify themselves and making excuses. By simply agreeing with the accurate criticism, they take the wind out of the sails of the criticism. They also stand a better chance of having a pleasant outcome with an adult if they both acknowledge and apologize for actions that were mistaken.

The Mea Culpa is a way of dealing with accurate criticism head-on. It's simply an admission, saying, "You're right, I did do that" or "That was my fault, I shouldn't have done that" or "That was a dumb thing to do." Even better is for children to learn to give apologies with the Mea Culpa. An apology can do wonders to reduce the effects of a confrontation involving criticism that's accurate. It's also valuable for children, as part of their human development, to learn the value and importance of offering sincere apologies.

Whenever my children get defensive with me or start making excuses when I'm justifiably correcting them, I remind them that they don't need to go through all that. I want them simply to use the Mea Culpa and apologize; then I use my own Power I and tell them what I want them to do by way of correction.

If you find that your children are getting all too good at the Mea Culpa, in other words, they keep repeating the same undesired behaviors and artfully use the Mea Culpa to weasel out of responsibility, then it's time for some strong corrective assistance. Sit down and have a Solution Time (see Chapter 6) with them to develop a simple plan with clear consequences to help them overcome their behavior.

Script to Introduce the Mea Culpa

Sometimes when people blame us for something, what they say is true. For example, they might say we've been teasing, or we broke something, or we were mean—and what they say is correct—we've done those things. Even though we're worthwhile creations of God, this doesn't mean that we always do good, or that we don't make mistakes. Blame can't change our goodness, but it can correctly point out things we've done that aren't good. The Mea Culpa is how we answer people when they correctly blame us for something we've done. Mea culpa means "my fault" in Latin. With the Mea Culpa you simply tell the truth and agree with what they're saying, by saying something like "You're right, I did do that" or "You're right, that was a mistake." By using the Mea Culpa you don't need to argue, or get defensive, or make excuses. If harm has been done, we expect you to apologize and make up for the mistake. We also expect you to change your ways if you're getting in the habit of doing harmful or unkind things. It's okay to make mistakes, but it's not okay to get in the habit of doing harmful things.

I want you always to tell me the truth about your mistakes by using the Mea Culpa with me. If I get angry when you admit to a mistake, you need to remind me that we have a deal—you'll always try to tell me the truth, and I'll always try to be fair and reasonable when you admit your mistakes.

Let's practice the Mea Culpa together. Let's say all the

following blaming statements that I make are true—at least in terms of what you've actually done. Use the Mea Culpa, which means just tell the truth, agree with my statements, and apologize if harm has been done. Also use the Power I and the Squeaky Wheel if I keep pushing you. Remember, there's no need to make excuses, just agree and apologize.

Practicing the Mea Culpa Together:

Role-Playing Examples

Feel free to substitute your own age-relevant wording.

Parent: You got home late again, what's your problem?

Child: You're right, I apologize for that.

Parent: Yeah, well you better change that routine.

Child: I know, I'm really sorry, it won't happen again.

Parent: Let's say I'm your teacher, and I say, "Your desk is a mess; you always seem to leave a mess."

Child: You're right, it is a mess.

Parent: Well, make sure you start cleaning things up.

Child: That's a good idea, I'll try better next time.

Parent: Let's say I'm your brother, and I come in and say, "Look, you ate the last of the cereal, what's your problem?"

Child: You're right, I did eat the last of the cereal.

Parent: Yeah, well maybe you should think more about others.

Child: You're probably right.

Parent: Let's say I'm your neighbor and you broke my window playing baseball, and I say, "Hey, you just broke my window.

Child: Yeah, I did, and I'm really sorry. I'll pay for it.

Parent: Well, you need to be a lot more careful; that window cost a lot of money.

Child: You're right, and I'm really sorry.

Parent: Well, your parents aren't going to be too happy about this.

Child: I know it, I'm really sorry.

Technique 6: Mighty Might

We've all had people in our lives (maybe even parents) who've learned the art of using blame as a tool for inducing guilt. "How could you possibly do that?" "You should know better than that." "Can't you think of anybody other than yourself?" We've all been there and maybe even have done that. The Mighty Might is a powerful technique that can be used to defend ourselves in those kinds of situations. It's particularly helpful when people use blame that's filled with "should" speech—like "You should know better" or "You should be ashamed of yourself" or "You should act your age." Sometimes criticism is accurate, and sometimes it's inaccurate. Likewise, sometimes it's used maturely to help kids change undesired behavior, and sometimes it's used immaturely to exact emotional punishment.

The Mighty Might is a deflective verbal technique that can empower children to respond to any verbal situation where criticism or judgmental comments they receive are meant to make them feel ashamed or to belittle and condemn them.

The Mighty Might is implemented simply by using a statement such as "You might (or could) be right" or "That might (or could) be so" over and over until the condemnation ceases. In essence, the statement is used to fight mean-spirited, condemning blame with flexible, deflective responses. Such responses are meant to nip in the bud an unfruitful verbal cycle by neither agreeing nor disagreeing with the mean statements or questions of the people who are blaming or teasing. The Mighty Might can also be used when we might basically disagree with parts of people's opinions, but don't have the time or energy to really get into a discussion.

Sometimes we might disagree with the "should" type of blame so much that it's just too hard simply to deflect it with the Mighty Might. If somebody uses "should" blaming that we find too hard to just disregard, we can always use the Power I and say we disagree, or we can use the Simple Question "why?," which we've already learned.

Script to Introduce the Mighty Might

The Mighty Might is a technique that can be used in a lot of tough verbal situations. It's especially good to use when people are blaming or teasing us. Sometimes people use blame to try to make us feel bad. With the Mighty Might you neither agree nor disagree with the blame. Instead, you use statements or words like "You might be right" or "You could be right" or "maybe" or "possibly," then you simply shrug the conversation off. Rather than get into an argument, or try to answer their criticism, you simply leave them with nothing else to say.

Let's practice the Mighty Might together. I'm going to give you some mean blame that's meant to try to make you feel bad. You respond with the Mighty Might, and use the Power I and the Squeaky Wheel if you need to.

Practicing the Mighty Might Together:

Role-Playing Examples

Feel free to substitute your own age-relevant wording.

Parent: Let's say I'm a kid at school and I start ragging on your basketball skills by saying, "Gee, can't you make any of your shots?"

Child: You might be right.

Parent: I might be right? I am right. Just look at your shots.

Child: You might be right.

Parent: Is that all you've got to say, "You might be right"?

Child: You might be right.

Parent: Let's say I'm a baseball coach and I say, "We're never going to win if you don't start getting some hits."

Child: You might be right.

Parent: Yeah, well you could use an attitude adjustment too.

Child: You might be right.

Parent: Okay, kid, I get your point.

Child: You might be right.

Parent: Let's say your brother starts getting mad at you because you won't go get something out of the refrigerator for him, and he says, "Go get it for me, you little baby."

Child: No, I don't want to.

Parent: You're so lame, I can't stand you.

Child: You might be right.

Parent: You are!

Child: Maybe.

Parent: Let's say another kid at school starts laughing at you and says, "Gee, your clothes look like they're from the seventies, you should get some new clothes."

Child: You might be right.

Parent: I am right, how could you wear that kind of stuff?

Child: You might be right.

Parent: Hey, get a life, kid.

Child: Maybe I will.

"Why?"

Parent: Sometimes people blame or tease us with "should" statements, like "You should never do that" or "You should really know better." If you feel strongly that they're wrong, just using the Mighty Might may not feel right for you. In those cases ask them the Simple Question "why?" which we've already learned. Let's just practice "why?" a few times. I'm going to give you some "should" blame statements, and you use "why?" or "why not?" or "why is that bad?" types of questions along with the Power I. Remember to use the Squeaky Wheel if I won't give up.

Parent: You really shouldn't talk so much.

Child: Why?

Parent: Because people get tired of hearing you.

Child: Why?

Parent: Just because.

Child: But why?

Parent: You really should wear your hair differently.

Child: Why?

Parent: Because it makes you look too young.

Child: Why is that bad?

Parent: You don't want to look so young, do you?

Child: Why not?

Parent: You should be more serious and not act so goofy.

Child: Why?

Parent: Because you're just too old to be acting this way.

Child: Why?

Parent: Just because it's so childish!

Child: Why?

Technique 7: Sorry Charlie

Then there are those great moments when we don't mince words. Sometimes the blame and opinions of others simply aren't worthy of too much attention—and the Mighty Might works just fine. But sometimes blame is simply and clearly false, and we need to respond. The Sorry Charlie is the reverse of the Mea Culpa. Instead of "You're right, I did do that," it's "You're wrong, I didn't do that." This doesn't need to be expressed in a defensive manner, just matter-of-factly. Whereas the Mea Culpa and the Mighty Might are more deflective verbal tools, the Sorry Charlie is more like an assertive counterpunch. Children sometimes are willing simply to slough off setting the record straight, figuring it's not worth the bother, especially with adults or other authority figures. However, it can be very important to set the record straight, both to correct false impressions and to teach people that they can't get away with any old, invalid, lazy, emotionally charged claim.

The Sorry Charlie becomes especially valuable in a home where children have gotten comfortable using the Mea Culpa. When they find that they can tell the truth about their mistakes without additional punishment, they don't have the incentive to lie. They trust us not to overreact when they honestly admit to mistakes, and we trust them when they correct us about something they've been blamed for. Children and parents alike need to understand that their relationships are much more enjoyable and simple when honesty and trust flow freely.

Script to Introduce the Sorry Charlie

Sometimes blame is false—we get blamed for things we didn't do. It's important that we don't just shrug off this false blame. If we shrug it off, people may get in the habit of wrongly blaming us, and they can develop ideas about us that are completely false. This may not be important with people we hardly know. But it's very important with people we're around a lot—including family. We need to set the record straight with them so that they don't blame us and don't develop false beliefs about us. We need to teach people how we want to be treated. The Sorry Charlie is just saying very clearly, "(Sorry Charlie) You're wrong about that" or "That's not correct."

I want there always to be a lot of trust between us. So if you tell me a Sorry Charlie, I'm going to believe you.

But your side of the deal is that you need to honestly admit when you've made a mistake that I ask you about, by using the Mea Culpa.

To practice the Sorry Charlie, I'm going to make some blame statements to you, and let's say they're not true. I want you to use the Sorry Charlie by telling me that I'm wrong and why I'm wrong. Also use the Power I and the Squeaky Wheel if you need to.

Practicing the Sorry Charlie Together:

Role-Playing Examples

Feel free to substitute your own age-relevant wording.

Parent: Let's say I'm a teacher at school and I say, "You got your homework in late again."

Child: No, actually you're wrong, I got my homework in on time.

Parent: It was supposed to be in before class, not after.

Child: Actually, I did put it on your desk before class.

Parent: I would have seen it.

Child: All I know is that I put it there.

Parent: Let's say I'm a kid at school, and I come up and you're already working on a computer, and I say, "Hey, it's my turn to use the computer."

Child: No, actually it's my turn until eleven o'clock.

Parent: No way, you've been on here for a long time.

Child: No, actually you're wrong; I haven't been on that long, and I'm going to be here until eleven o'clock.

Parent: You know, you're really a dork.

Child: You might be right.

Parent: Let's say I'm the principal at school, and I say, "I heard you were picking on some kids after school."

Child: No, that's wrong, I wasn't picking on anyone.

Parent: Well, there were other kids there who saw it.

Child: All I can tell you is that I didn't pick on any kids.

Parent: But some other kids saw this happening.

Child: Well, then they're wrong.

Parent: Let's say I come home one evening and I say, "Somebody marked up my car with a bad scratch."

Child: It wasn't me.

Parent: It had to be you. It's right next to where you put your bike.

Child: It wasn't me.

Parent: It had to be you.

Child: It wasn't.

Parent: Let's say I'm a kid at school and I say, "Hey, you took my skateboard."

Child: No, I didn't take it.

Parent: Yes, you did, give it back to me.

Child: No, you're wrong. I never had it.

Parent: I think you're lying.

Child: I'm not. I never had your skateboard.

CHAPTER THREE

The Way of the Hummingbird: Responding to Teasing

Hummingbirds are both the smallest birds in the world and perhaps the most fearless. Although generally friendly, they have been known to attack humans, dogs, and cats encroaching on their space, as well as crows and even hawks. For this reason the Navajos ranked them alongside wolves and mountain lions for their courage. The Way of the Hummingbird is the way of responding to teasing by others—even if they're bigger.

It's clear that if children had the same finely tuned nerve endings as parents, there would be a lot less teasing in the world. As it is, they don't. At the end of an exhausting day, my wife asked my son if he really enjoyed hearing the "wailing and gnashing of teeth" of his siblings when he teased them. His response was "Actually, I kind of do." Thus the dilemma.

By nature some kids love to tease. Whether teasing is gentle and fun (as in the case of friends teasing each other) or is meant to be belittling and mean (as is sometimes the case with older siblings teasing younger siblings), it is always meant to get a reaction. Between friends it's usually meant to get a grin or a laugh. Between siblings it's frequently meant to get a tear or a cry from a younger family member. Children need to develop the skill to deal successfully with the type of teasing that is meant to ridicule and demean them.

Two techniques that can be used in responding to teasing have already been introduced: the Power I and the Mighty Might. As in any situation where kids are being bothered by others, it's good for them to get in the habit of telling people directly how they feel and what they want. They should understand that when they're being teased the Power I (direct communication) is the place to start. However, really belligerent teasers usually aren't deterred by the direct requests of their victims. They aren't satisfied until they get the reaction they're looking for. Your children have already learned one technique that they can use when the Power I doesn't work: the Mighty Might. In the same way this technique is used with blamers, who are trying to exact emotional punishment, it can be used with teasers, who are trying to exact emotional pain. A response of "You might be right" can deflect virtually any type of teasing. If continuous Mighty Might responses are followed up with determined Squeaky Wheel efforts, most teasers will become discouraged.

Children need to develop the skill to deal successfully with the type of teasing that is meant to ridicule and demean them.

The Way of the Hummingbird introduces three additional techniques that can be used to respond to teasers. Kids need to understand that any of these techniques may require a determined Squeaky Wheel effort to be successful. They also need to know that *showing* that they're not upset by the teasers is as important as the words they use. Mastery of these techniques can provide greater peace to child and parent alike.

I have to admit that I was one of those kids who enjoyed teasing other kids, so it may be genetic (I still enjoy teasing other adults from time to time). I can relate somewhat to the glee on my teenager's face after he's successfully teased his brother or sister. But relating to it doesn't mean tolerating it. I require Kind Talk (see Chapter 5), and I intervene with a Solution Time (see Chapter 4) if unwanted teasing continues. While it's important for my younger children to practice the tools to respond to teasing and become verbally tough, I believe it's even more important to maintain a culture of baseline dignity and respect in the home. Chronic teasing can have negative long-term consequences for children if left unchecked.

SCRIPT TO INTRODUCE THE WAY OF THE HUMMINGBIRD

Even though hummingbirds are the smallest birds in the world, they're also the bravest. They're usually very friendly, but they've been known to attack humans, dogs, cats, and hawks who are too close to their space. The Navajos ranked them alongside wolves and mountain lions for their courage. The way the hummingbird responds to much bigger creatures is a good symbol to remind us of how we can respond to others who tease us when we don't like it. The Way of the Hummingbird is the way of responding to teasing.

We've already learned two techniques that can be used to respond to teasing: the Power I and the Mighty Might. We're going to review those techniques and how to use them with teasing situations. Then I'm going to teach you three new techniques that you can use to deal with teasing.

Power I and Mighty Might in Response to Teasing

Script to Introduce the Power I and the Mighty Might in Teasing Situations

You've already learned two techniques that can be used to deal with teasers, the Power I and the Mighty Might. If somebody is teasing you and you don't like it, the best place to start is always the Power I. It's good to tell people directly how you feel and what you want. You can say things like "I want you to stop bugging me" or "I really don't like you to do that." If they won't stop be loud by yelling "Stop it" or "Cut it out." You can also ask strong Simple Questions like "What's your problem?" or "Who asked you?" Stand tall and give them an angry face if you need to. People who respect your wishes will stop, although you may need to use the Squeaky Wheel.

If they don't stop, you can use the Mighty Might. If you're persistent they should give up at some point, because you'll be taking all the fun out of their teasing. You need to remember that people usually tease in order to get a reaction. And people who are teasing to be mean want a reaction that shows you're unhappy. The Mighty Might gives them a reaction that isn't fun for them.

I'm going to pretend that I'm an older kid teasing you, and I want you just to keep responding to me using the Power I and the Mighty Might.

Practicing the Power I and the Mighty Might Together in Teasing Situations:

Role-Playing Examples

Feel free to substitute your own age-relevant wording.

Parent: Hey, Shorty, what's your problem?

Child: I don't want you to call me that.

Parent: What's the matter, Shorty, you don't like it?

Child: You might be right.

Parent: I *am* right, Shorty.

Child: You might be.

Parent: Well, if you're not short, at least you're funny-looking.

Child: Knock it off, you're bugging me.

Parent: Well, just look in the mirror.

Child: You might be right.

Parent: Is all you can say is "You might be right"?

Child: You might be right.

Parent: I figure only baby-type kids say, "You might be right."

Child: You might be right.

Parent: Why don't you go cry to your parents?

Child: You might be right.

Parent: Hey, give it up.

Child: Maybe I should.

Parent: Your parents probably think you're a wimp anyway.

Child: Hey, I'd really like you to lay off, that stuff gets annoying.

Parent: What, you mean like calling you a wimp?

Child: Yeah, I don't like it.

Parent: Well, you are one, what can I do?

Child: You might be right.

Technique 8: The Shrug

When it comes down to it, people with the most tranquility in their lives may be not the ones who are serenely secluded in temples of meditation but rather the ones who can deal with the hustle and bustle of life with a shrug. Not only are they peaceful inside but they also get important things done out in the world.

The Shrug can be used in all teasing situations and is simple to implement. But it also requires a verbal and internal discipline that isn't always easy for children to maintain emotionally. The Shrug means simply mentally, physically, and verbally shrugging teasing off. In order to get used to doing the Shrug, it's helpful to get in the practice of physically shrugging the shoulders, looking away, acting bored, and saying, "I don't care" or "So what." It's important for children to stop any visual contact with the teaser. If children can master this technique in their everyday lives, they probably won't need any other technique to deal with teasing. And learning to shrug off teasing may help them to shrug off other irritations in life as well.

Script to Introduce the Shrug

There's one sure way to respond to teasing, and that's to shrug it off. You simply shrug your shoulders and say, "I don't care," or "So what," either out loud or in your mind, then walk away. You also stop looking at the teasers. Teasers would love to have you look at them and their smiles and gestures as they tease you. But don't do it—just look bored and walk away. If you watch sports on TV, you'll notice that there are some great athletes, like Michael Jordan and Jerry Rice, who get teased by others, and they just smile and walk away without paying any attention. They're doing the Shrug.

When I was a kid I used to get teased sometimes. I know it's not fun. But I also know that the worst thing you can do is act hurt or upset. Try not to do that—just act bored, smile, or walk away.

I'm going to pretend that I'm another kid teasing you, and I want you to do the Shrug by shrugging your shoulders, looking away, acting bored, and saying "I don't care," or "So what," either out loud or in your mind.

Practicing the Shrug Together:

Role-Playing Examples

Feel free to substitute your own age-relevant wording.

Parent: Hey, how come you look so small?

Child: [With a shrug] I don't care.

Parent: Hey, you walk kind of funny.

Child: [With a shrug] So what.

Parent: That shirt you have on looks dorky, how come you're wearing it?

Child: [With a shrug] I don't care.

Parent: Hey, can't you even read a book yet?

Child: [With a shrug] So what.

Technique 9: Reverse Tease

We've all witnessed the power of wisecracking class clowns. With one little quip they can humble the mighty and proud. People like David Letterman and Rosie O'Donnell are able to use this power to humble the mighty and proud at a very high level. As with most personality traits, there's something to be learned from this wisecracking talent. Harnessing a little bit of it can reap great rewards for adults and children alike.

Whether kids are talented smart alecks or not, a fun approach to responding to teasing can be to use sarcastic humor. Sarcasm has a negative connotation that isn't entirely deserved. For sure, sarcasm can be biting and mean-spirited, used to humiliate or cruelly ridicule someone else. But it can also be humorous and playful, used to poke fun in a gentle way. The Reverse Tease employs the playful type of sarcasm to respond to teasers. It's not simply teasing back in the same manner that the teasing has been given (as in the "I know you are, but what am I" mode). Rather, it's responding with humor and comic exaggeration. In response to teasing, a child says something like "Oh, thank you, thank you very much" or "You're so kind" or "You know, I think you're right" or "You know, my great dream is to be just like you." It can take the form of fake crying or politely bowing (for example, if somebody makes fun of and laughs at a physical mishap). The point is that instead of fighting the teasing, the child pokes fun at it, by responding to it in some humorous, exaggerated way.

This is one of my children's favorite techniques to role-play. They have a lot of fun practicing it with each other. But it's clearly best suited for older children, unless you have a younger child who is blessed with natural wit.

Script to Introduce the Reverse Tease

Sometimes it's fun to tease teasers right back by going along with their gags. You can do this by agreeing with the teasers in a funny, sarcastic way. You can say things like "Oh, you're so right, I just wish I were more like you" or "Oh, thank you for being so thoughtful" or "Oh, please, don't hurt my feelings." You can also use gestures like bowing or faking that you're crying. If you've ever seen people like David Letterman or Rosie O'Donnell on TV, you'll notice that they use the Reverse Tease all the time.

I'm going to pretend that I'm a kid teasing you, and I want you to use the Reverse Tease on me by agreeing with me, or teasing right back, in a funny kind of a way. Remember that this isn't something you'd ever use with teasers who are really mean and might physically hurt you. With those types of teasers you use the Disappearing Act, which is the next technique.

Practicing the Reverse Tease Together:

Role-Playing Examples

Feel free to substitute your own age-relevant wording.

Parent: Hey, what's your problem, don't you know how to walk?

Child: You're just too kind.

Parent: Yeah, well, you look like a penguin when you walk.

Child: Thanks, I've always wanted to be a penguin.

Parent: Just look in the mirror, you've become one.

Child: Oh my gosh, you're right, call my parents!

Parent: You're not very popular around here, kid. What's your problem?

Child: I don't know, I just wish I were as popular as you.

Parent: Maybe it's because you have a big nose.

Child: This nose is in the Guinness world record book, I'll have you know.

Parent: Who taught you how to play basketball, your grandmother?

Child: You know, actually, old Granny did.

Parent: It looks like it.

Child: She actually had some pretty good moves for being ninety-two.

Parent: Why don't you grow up and stop acting like a baby?

Child: That's impossible, I *am* a baby, a very large one, but I'm still a baby.

Parent: Yeah, well, you sure act like one.

Child: True; just give me a few years, and I'll be a big boy like you.

Technique 10: Disappearing Act

Children need to be careful with potentially dangerous teasers who have the possibility of doing them real physical harm. With such people the less said the better. There is one sure way of dealing with this type of teaser, or any other teaser or annoyance, for that matter, and that's simply to get up and disappear (leave). Sometimes, when patience runs thin, or other verbal techniques aren't working, or there is the potential for physical confrontation, nothing works like quickly disappearing. Children also need to be taught that when they disappear, they need to go where there are responsible adults around who could help them if necessary. They shouldn't go anyplace where a dangerous bully could catch up with them and be alone with them.

We need to make it clear to our children that they need to tell school authorities and us if they're being picked on by a bully. This isn't tattling. This is standing up for their rights. They have the right to safe access to education. What adults would allow themselves to be assaulted or have their property destroyed and not stand up for their personal rights?

It's also good to remind children, just as they're taught in school, that they need to do the Disappearing Act when approached by strangers. Children have to understand that sometimes the most assertive thing they can do is simply get up and leave.

Script to Introduce the Disappearing Act

Not all people are the same. While people are born good, some become mean and do bad things. Sometimes people can be dangerous, and their teasing is meant to start trouble where somebody can get hurt. Whenever you think that this might be happening, you need to just disappear from the situation. You need to quietly and quickly leave without saying anything—just disappear, and take your friends with you. And make sure that you quickly get to a place where there are helpful adults—like teachers, neighbors we know, parents, or other older people. You shouldn't be shy about asking these adults for help. You don't want to have bullies follow you to a place where you're alone with them. It's very important that you tell your teachers and me if you're being picked on by bullies.

This isn't tattling—this is standing up for your rights. You have the right not to be bullied. Do bullies ever bother you? Tell me about it.

The Disappearing Act can also be used when you simply don't want to deal with any type of situation any longer. As you've learned from school, it's especially important to do the Disappearing Act when you're approached by strangers.

To practice the Disappearing Act, I'm going to pretend like I'm a mean kid teasing you, and you respond by disappearing. This means you just get up and leave. Remember not to look at me or respond to what I'm saying; just get up and leave.

Practicing the Disappearing Act Together

Give your child a variety of threatening teasing phrases and have him or her practice simply getting up and disappearing from the scene, without saying anything or acknowledging anything.

Note to Parents: Various studies suggest that 15 percent of students are either bullied regularly or are initiators of bullying behavior. This is a lot of kids. If your children are being bothered by bullies who threaten them with physical harm, it's clearly time to intervene. It's time for you to assertively express yourself to the parents of bullies or to school administrators and teachers. We need to demand that our schools have strong antibullying programs in place. A good resource to help you and your school to initiate such a program is *Childhood Bullying and Teasing: What School Personnel, Other Professionals and Parents Can Do* (by Dorothea M. Ross, published by the American Counseling Association in 1996).

Responding Artfully to Teasing Questions

Questions that are meant to tease can be especially troubling for kids, who are accustomed to trying to answer questions. When the question is really meant to ridicule rather than to get information, kids can be a little bewildered. They can directly use the Power I, as in "I don't want to answer your question" or "I don't want you to tease me." They can always use the Shrug or the Disappearing Act and not respond at all. They can use the Mighty Might to deflect the question. If they're older, they can use the Reverse Tease by responding to a teasing question with a goofy, sarcastic answer.

Additionally, a quick response that can be used in most situations is *"Because I want to,"* a simple adaptation of the Power I. Examples: "How come you're wearing that ugly dress?" *"Because I want to."* "Why are you so small?" *"Because I want to be."* "How come you always play with little baby dolls?" *"Because I want to."* "How come you have those funny green eyes?" *"Because I want them."*

Script to Practice Responding Artfully to Teasing Questions

Sometimes kids might ask you questions for which they don't really want answers, they just want to tease you. They might ask things like "Where did you get that funny-looking nose?" or "How come you're so short?" or "Why do you always act like a baby?" You need to remember that you never have to answer questions you don't want to. You especially don't need to answer questions that are meant to tease. We've learned several verbal techniques that you can use if you're asked teasing questions:

The Power I can be used by saying things like "I don't want you to tease me" or "I don't answer questions like that."

The Mighty Might can be used by just repeating "You might be right."

The Shrug can be used by just shrugging, saying, "I don't care," or "So what" and getting up and leaving.

The Reverse Tease can be used by answering a teasing question with a really funny, goofy answer.

The Disappearing Act can be used by just getting up and leaving.

Also, you can always answer a teasing question by saying, "Because I want to." "Because I want to" is just the Power I with a "because" in front of it. You could also say things like "Because I like it" or "Because I felt like it." It's good to get used to saying "Because I want to" or "Because I like it" in response to questions. Just because people ask us questions, we don't have to answer them with anything more than "Because I want to."

Here are some examples of using "Because I want to."

"Because I Want To . . ."

How come you . . . ? Because I want to.

Why are you so . . . ? Because I want to be.

Why did you . . . ? Because I wanted to.

Where did you get that . . . ? I got it from . . . because I like it.

What is that weird . . . ? It's a . . . and I have it because I like it.

Aren't you acting a little too . . . ? Maybe, but only because I want to.

Let's practice some situations where another kid is asking you some teasing questions. The first time we go through, practice answering them using "Because I want to" or "Because I like it." The second time, I'll ask you the same questions and you practice using other verbal techniques.

Practicing Responding to Teasing Questions Together:

Role-Playing Examples

Feel free to substitute your own age-relevant wording.

Parent: Hey, how come you've got such big, ugly feet?

Child: Because I want them.

Parent: Don't you think you act a little babyish for your age?

Child: Maybe, but only because I want to.

Parent: Where did you get that funny-looking shirt?

Child: I got it from the store because I like it.

Parent: How come you're always so slow when you run?

Child: Because I want to.

Parent: Why do you always talk with your mouth full of food?

Child: Because I want to.

Parent: Why do you always wear the same thing?

Child: Because I like to.

CHAPTER FOUR

The Way of the Dove: Resolving Conflicts

Doves are very gentle birds. Their soft coo is one of the most pleasant sounds in nature. They perch in tranquillity and gracefully flutter from one branch to another. For centuries the dove has been a symbol of peace and reconciliation for Judaism, Christianity, and Islam. Much of the lack of peace in the world is the result of people using conflict to solve their problems. The Way of the Dove is the way of achieving peace through successfully resolving conflicts.

Many of us were amazingly patient before we had kids. In those innocent, heady days we were shocked by the impatience of our friends who had children. Why couldn't they just use the simple, loving parenting techniques that we had read about while waiting in the dentist's office? What was wrong with these people? How could they allow and even participate in conflict in their homes? Then we had our own children, and everything changed. Nothing could have prepared us for a child's innate ability to probe and expose our points of weakness. We scrambled for books and magazine articles, but to little avail. Sooner or later the fighting, teasing, and whining would get to even the best of us (except for the very best). Eventually we would give in to this Chinese water torture, the dam would break, and we would cascade into the fray ourselves.

Whether at the level of nations, companies, families, or kids in the school yard, conflict is the result of a failure to find reasonable solutions to problems. With really belligerent people, conflict is frequently unavoidable. When these types of people want harmful things to happen at all costs, without compromise, only conflict will stop them. But more often, conflict occurs because people get overwhelmed by emotion and can't think in a cooperative and reasonable way.

A conflict is both a type of response to a problem and a special problem in and of itself. It's a problem of two or more people becoming obstacles to each other in getting what they want.

A certain amount of conflict in human relations is normal and to be expected. People have their own needs and opinions, and sometimes they have to stand up for themselves and represent themselves in verbally strong ways. But a habit of conflict can corrode the happiness and solidarity of family life. Sometimes people fight just to fight. As the adults in the home, we have to provide leadership in resolving conflict. We have to set an example. We also can't simply let "kids be kids" and allow them to pick on each other in mean ways. Children who learn to solve their differences with others through conflict grow up to be the adults who solve their differences through conflict. For people who want to change the world, teaching children how to resolve conflict successfully is a great place to start.

Conflict can corrode the happiness and solidarity of family life. As the adults in the home, we have to provide leadership in resolving conflict.

Much childhood conflict is a result of blame and teasing. I've already discussed verbal techniques that can help children deal with blame and teasing. But sometimes blame and teasing don't stop, and sometimes conflict is based on other problems. The Way of the Dove is made up of techniques to deal with any type of conflict that won't go away. The first two techniques, Solution Time and the Coin Toss, provide processes by which children can sit down and solve their differences. Conflict resolution is fundamentally a creative search for solutions, but children must get into a solution-oriented mode before they can start to think creatively. The third technique, Cone of Silence, is used to mitigate the harmful effects of conflict when it's already gotten to a difficult, overheated stage. This is done by implementing and maintaining a formal cooling-off period. The Cone of Silence is an important safety valve to ensure that conflict doesn't become an accepted part of a family's culture.

SCRIPT TO INTRODUCE THE WAY OF THE DOVE

Part of life includes conflict. Conflict is arguing and fighting. Sometimes we have conflict in our family. Some conflict is natural and normal. If two people want different things, they may try to stand up strongly for what they want. And if people want something that's really important to them, sometimes they have to fight to get it. A big part of standing up for ourselves is learning to tell people exactly how we feel and what we want.

But conflict is not the best way for people to solve their differences. If conflict happens too often or is too mean, it can be very harmful. War is an example of how terrible conflict can be. Peace is what comes when we learn to talk through and solve our differences rather than fight over them.

The Way of the Dove is the way of peace—the way of finding solutions to our differences and conflicts. The Way of the Dove is made up of techniques that can help us resolve conflicts.

Technique 11: Solution Time 1

The purpose of Solution Time is to help children learn the basic steps for developing solutions to conflicts. Solution Time is essentially a time-out—a time-out from conflict and a time-in toward creative problem solving. It forces everyone (including parents) to slow down and talk in more reasonable tones. The goal is to move children from the mode of blindly fighting for their own way toward negotiating a way that accommodates the reasonable interests of all parties. Until children become familiar with the Solution Time format, parents need to play a strong mediation/mentoring role. This involves calling for Solution Time and seeing that the following rules are enforced:

1. Each child must come and sit down.
2. Only one person can speak at a time.
3. Each side gets a chance to fully give his or her experience of the conflict (especially how each side *feels*), without interruption from the other side.
4. Each side must come up with at least one possible solution; if they don't, the other side's solution automatically prevails.
5. The parent helps the parties to generate solution options.
6. At the end of generating solutions, a vote is taken on the solutions.
7. If there's no consensus on a solution, then get agreement on the best way to make the deci-

sion without agreement, such as flipping a coin, choosing numbers, neither being able to have what he or she wants, and so on.

8. If this fails, the parent needs to act as judge and choose which of the options seems most fair.
9. A consequence must also be agreed to in the event that either party doesn't live up to his or her part of the solution.

As children become trained in these steps, parents should have them go through as many of the steps as possible by themselves, only helping to initiate and conclude the process as needed.

I've developed the habit of really prodding my children to come up with solutions when they present me with conflict problems (or any other types of problems). There's a balance to be maintained. You want your children to feel comfortable telling you how they feel about things—so you need to listen patiently to their problems first. But for their long-term benefit, they really need to get in the habit of going through the difficult work of coming up with solutions rather than simply raising problems. You can help them come up with ideas, but they need to develop their own ideas and decisions.

Script to Introduce Solution Time

A conflict is a special kind of problem. It's a problem where people fight over getting their own way.

Sometimes kids have conflict because they blame or tease each other and just won't stop. We've already talked about how to deal with blame and teasing. But other times kids have conflicts because they want to have the same thing at the same time or they want the other person to do something. When you're with your brother or sister or friends, you might have conflicts with them or they might have conflicts with each other. Solution Time is a good tool to use in helping to solve conflicts.

Solution Time is a time-out from conflict where people have to stop their fighting and figure out a solution to their differences. When you're in the middle of an argument here at home, you need to call for a Solution Time. If you don't call for one, I will. During Solution Time we'll figure out a solution to the conflict. We'll get everybody's side of the story, and then we'll try to figure out a solution that's fair.

Sometimes when you're away from home you might get into conflicts that you'll need to help solve. Try to offer solutions that work for both sides. Have the other side offer their solutions. Offer to flip a coin if you can't easily agree. Get help from your teacher if you need to. Remember that if conflicts look like they might get dangerous, immediately leave (do the Disappearing Act; see Chapter 3), and tell an adult. When you're in a position to help others solve their conflicts, the first step is to call for a time-out: Solution Time. Each person should be allowed to take a turn and tell his or her side of the story. There shouldn't be interruptions. Once each person has told his or her side, you should figure out the following:

Conflict Resolution Steps

1. Find out what each side really wants and how each side feels about the situation.
2. Have each side come up with possible solutions.
3. Come up with solutions that will make it possible for each side to get part or all of what they want.
4. If neither side wants to budge, determine what fair way can be used to make a decision: flipping a coin, taking turns, asking an adult to help make the decision.

If I'm around, and you can't solve your conflict on your own, I'll help you solve it. I'll listen to both sides, and both sides will have to come up with at least one reasonable solution that could work for both. If one side doesn't give me a solution idea, then I'll automatically go with the other solution. If we can't come to a solution that both sides agree on, then I'll use my best judgment to come up with one for you.

But remember that the first, most important step is simply to stop the fighting and arguing and sit down to have Solution Time.

Solution Time is taught by calling for a Solution Time whenever there is unreasonable conflict. Simply call the conflicting parties together and go through the steps just outlined. Let them solve the conflict as much as possible, providing guidance and ideas as necessary.

Technique 12: Coin Toss

For kids, coins are magic. Coins can buy a lot of bubble gum, they feel nice and substantial in your pocket, and you can find them every so often just lying around. Coins can also be magic in resolving conflict.

The Coin Toss is a get-to-the-quick Solution Time. Besides blame and teasing, a lot of childhood conflict is centered on either two children wanting the same thing at the same time or one child wanting the other one to do something or to stop doing something. Solution Time can ultimately be used to come up with a solution to any of these types of conflicts. But children shouldn't have to go through Solution Time every time there's a simple problem involving taking turns or sharing or deciding who does what. It's very healthy for children and adults alike to learn to deal with such issues of cooperation in a give-and-take manner. The Coin Toss is the everyday alternative that we've grown up with but probably don't use enough. It's a ready-made solution that can be applied any time we need to decide who goes first, who does what, what we share—it's as much a mental attitude as it is a physical process.

The Coin Toss is taught by prompting children to toss a coin (or pick a number) whenever a simple problem comes up. Whenever it's time for Solution Time, you can ask them if they prefer to do a full-fledged Solution Time or if a simple Coin Toss will suffice. This will help them to get in the habit of solving simple problems in a simple way.

Script to Introduce the Coin Toss

You can always use Solution Time to solve conflicts. However, sometimes it's easier just to do a Coin Toss. The Coin Toss means that if you have a conflict over sharing, taking turns, or anything else, you can quickly solve the problem by flipping a coin or picking a number. You've probably flipped a coin before to settle differences. It's a good way to solve differences that aren't really that important.

Whenever differences come up over sharing or taking turns, you can simply say something like "Let's flip a coin—the winner gets the first turn and then we'll change after half an hour."

Let's practice a few times. I'll give you some conflict situations, and you decide what a fair deal would be and tell me, "Let's flip for it." Then we'll actually flip for it.

Practicing the Coin Toss Together:

Role-Playing Examples

Feel free to substitute your own age-relevant wording.

Parent: Let's say you and I want to play with the same game at the same time. Give me a fair solution and a Coin Toss.

Child: One person will play with it first for thirty minutes, then trade back and forth every thirty minutes. Let's flip to see who goes first. (Coin Toss)

Parent: Let's say there are two chores to be done, washing the dishes and doing the laundry, and neither one of us wants to do them. Give me a fair solution and a Coin Toss.

Child: We'll toss a coin, and whoever wins can choose which chore to do. Let's flip to see who gets to choose. (Coin Toss)

Parent: Let's say you've been reading my favorite book for a long time and I want to read it now, but you want to finish. Give me a fair solution and a Coin Toss.

Child: We'll toss a coin, and if I win I finish the book, but if I lose you can read it now. (Coin Toss)

Parent: Let's say somebody needs to take out the garbage and nobody can remember whose turn it is. Give me a fair solution and a Coin Toss.

Child: We'll toss a coin, and whoever loses takes the turn now. Let's flip to see who has to take it out. (Coin Toss)

Technique 13: Cone of Silence

Okay, so sometimes fighting and arguing take on a life of their own. Bad feelings are so strong that Solution Time can't be wedged in. Adults don't always get along, so why should kids always be able to? As pointed out with teasing, sometimes the best verbal technique isn't verbal at all. Sometimes it's best to use silence. We all know that kids sometimes don't really want solutions, they really do want to tease, argue, and fight. It feels good to them to vent their anger and frustration. And their talk can get more unkind and uncivil as they tangle away.

In cases where all the patient, reasonable talk in the world doesn't seem to end conflict for more than a few moments, it's time for the ultimate technique—the Cone of Silence.

The Cone of Silence is another time-out of sorts. It's a time-out from kids being able to be together or speak to each other. It's a time-out for cooling off. Just as with Maxwell Smart in the old *Get Smart* TV series, the kids have a cone of silence placed around them (invisible in this case) that keeps them from talking to each other for fifteen minutes. If a child speaks while under the Cone of Silence, she or he needs to have a few more minutes added to the silence period or have some other predetermined consequence come into play.

Sometimes we need to place a Cone of Silence on ourselves as parents. It's only natural that the stresses of life make us feel cranky occasionally. But if we can't gain control in moments of stress, we can end up saying and doing very hurtful things. It's much better in those moments to walk away and take a breather rather than wreak the havoc that can come from uncontrolled anger. We're the adults. We need to restrain ourselves even if our children don't yet have that ability.

A Time-Together

I personally don't believe in the traditional time-out anymore. I much prefer a time-together. I simply tell my children, "Come and spend some time with me." So during a Cone of Silence I have them sit with me or near me, or have them ride with me in the car if I need to go someplace. In the case of two children, one can sit near me and the other can sit near my wife or go do something else (or also sit near me). I've found that this method is much more effective and kind than isolation. Instead of giving the kids "solitary confinement," I give them "rehab." If a basketball player is having a hard time in a game, you don't send him to the locker room, you have him come and sit next to you on the bench.

Script to Introduce the Cone of Silence

Sometimes people, both adults and children, get into fights that they can't stop very easily. They can't solve their conflicts because they can't seem to stop fighting. In those cases it's very good to have a time-out from each other—or something called a Cone of Silence. A Cone of Silence is where you can't be around each other or talk to each other for about fifteen minutes. I'll have you come and sit with me or near me during the Cone of Silence. This is a chance to calm down and get a breather. Hopefully after you've had a Cone of Silence, you can come back together and get along and solve your conflict by using a Solution Time. In the future I'm going to call for a Cone of Silence whenever we can't solve a fighting and arguing problem.

If you find yourself starting to get into a bad argument or fight at school, try real hard to place a Cone of Silence on yourself and walk away. It's better to just cool off rather than get in the middle of trouble. Deal with back talk the way the best athletes do—just smile and shrug it off.

In everyday life, as conflict becomes unkind and difficult to control, call for a Cone of Silence—a time-out from talking to each other and being around each other.

CHAPTER FIVE

The Way of the Blackbird: Confident Social Conversation

Blackbirds are among the most social birds in the world. They can gather in wintering flocks of mixed species that sometimes number in the millions of birds. If you stand in a field and observe a flock of blackbirds, it becomes immediately apparent how much they chatter and move among one another with ease. The Way of the Blackbird is the way of confidently having friendly social conversation with others.

I've always been intrigued by the behavior of young children when it comes to having company around. They can be so chatty in private and then immediately clam up when company arrives. They're suddenly politely bashful, no matter how rambunctious they had been just seconds before. If you prod them, slowly but surely they start to talk a little about themselves, maybe ask a few questions, and show a toy or two. A lot of them then move into a kind of goofy, show-off, look-what-I-can-do phase. And by the end of the evening they're hooting and hollering all through the house with complete abandon. They transform themselves from shy wallflowers into rowdy sailors in a saloon in all of about thirty minutes. This is another one of those wonderful mysteries of childhood.

Some children are naturally able to feel comfortable in social situations and strike up conversations from the initial point of contact. But many children are not. This can be a result of their inherent personality, their age, or their previous experience in such situations. The Way of the Blackbird is intended to give children tools that they can use to deal successfully with friendly social conversation.

There's nothing wrong with shyness. Some people are more shy than others from birth. Most of us have experienced situations where we feel shy. There's something endearing about children who are defiantly shy and are determined to stay within their comfort zones. But shyness can also get in the way of opportunities and self-fulfillment. It can impede full self-expression, contact with helpful people, and the higher level of enjoyment that can come from a calm outward focus toward others. The Way of the Blackbird provides tools to help expand children's comfort zones in situations where they need or want to have friendly social conversations. For a complete review of the issue of shyness, see *Shyness: What It Is and What to Do About It* (by Philip G. Zimbardo, published by Addison-Wesley in 1977).

Another important aspect of good social interchange involves speaking kindly to others. This aspect needs to be part of a family's culture whether a child is naturally shy or not. We can get into the strange habit of speaking more kindly to others than to members of our own family. It's not reasonable to expect children to be kind to each other all the time—but it's reasonable to expect it a lot of the time.

The Way of the Blackbird provides tools to help expand children's comfort zones in situations where they need or want to have friendly social conversations.

As with all the techniques in this book, modeling is a particularly powerful way to teach our children. In the case of social conversation, we're able to kill two toads (birds just wouldn't do for this book!) with one stone. We can sit down and have some good talks with our children and in the process give them practice with social conversation. It seems clear that good social conversation skills can be influenced by good, open (uncriticized) communication experience in the home.

SCRIPT TO INTRODUCE THE WAY OF THE BLACKBIRD

Blackbirds are birds that like to be with one another. Sometimes during the winter they gather in groups that can number in the millions. If you stand in a field and watch blackbirds walking around looking for food, you'll notice how much they chatter with one another. The Way of the Blackbird is learning to talk confidently with others when we want to.

There's nothing wrong with not talking to other people when you don't want to. But sometimes you might either need or want to talk to people, and it's good to have some ways of starting up conversations and keeping them going.

It's also good to speak kindly to people—especially in our own family. Speaking kindly means speaking to people in the way that we'd like to be spoken to. The Way of the Blackbird includes three techniques that can help us with friendly and kind conversation.

Technique 14: Sherlock Holmes

One of the most difficult problems for children in social situations is knowing what to say and where to begin conversations. There's one sure way of managing any social situation, and that's to ask questions, just like with Simple Questions. This requires going on a detective search to find out as much as you can about another person. Larry King maintains that one of the keys to being a successful conversationalist is simply to ask people about themselves or about what they think. "What do you think . . . ?" or "What's your opinion about . . . ?" can be great questions to encourage conversation. The idea of the Sherlock Holmes is to learn to ask questions of people and to really listen to their answers. Once you get hooked on discovering things about people and their life experiences, it's always easy to strike up a conversation. When children are quite young, they have an incredible ability to ask questions, so it's not difficult to rekindle the burning embers of this instinct. They have to learn to turn their interests out toward other people. In so doing they can free themselves from the inward focus that can make social situations less enjoyable.

Listening isn't always as natural as asking questions—and unfortunately we sometimes seem to listen less the older we get. Maybe the cardinal sin of parenthood is not listening with understanding. I believe that we automatically reduce our children's self-regard when we habitually don't listen to them or express general lack of interest in them and what they care about. We can tarnish our relationships with our children if we habitually jump to conclusions and don't try to understand things from their points of view.

There are basically two types of listening: (1) socially sympathetic and polite listening, which is used to be respectful and kind but is basically passive, and (2) truly investigative listening, which is very active mentally and is used to deeply understand and absorb something—the type of listening we do when we really perk up and strive to comprehend, asking plenty of questions, because something important is at stake. While there is a time and a place for both types of listening, the Sherlock Holmes requires the second type of active, investigative listening. We sometimes think if we don't talk, we're listening. To listen with understanding is to let go of ourselves and engage all of our attention in finding out about the other person.

It's particularly important to learn to ask follow-up questions. For example, if a child asks where somebody lives, the next questions might be why the person's family moved there, how the person likes it there, how long the person's lived there, what it's like to live there, and so forth. It's usually the follow-up questions that really help us understand each other.

Anytime we strike up a good, two-way conversation with our children, we're helping them develop social conversation skills. Anytime we engage them in group conversations when company is over, we're helping to build their social confidence.

Script to Introduce the Sherlock Holmes

Sometimes we may get into situations with adults or other kids where we want to just have a friendly talk but we don't know exactly how to start the conversation or how to keep it going. When you feel shy around people, try to remember that no matter who the people are, they're no better than you are—they're just people. You never need to feel like you have to talk to people, but when you would like to, you can use the Sherlock Holmes to help you out. The Sherlock Holmes is a technique to help you talk with anybody at any time.

Sherlock Holmes was a fictitious detective from England. One of his great talents was to ask lots of questions and to listen really well. The Sherlock Holmes means that you act like a detective. You ask people questions about themselves. You ask them what they think about things. You then listen carefully to how they answer and try to understand their thoughts and feelings. To listen means that you really pay attention to what people are saying and you try to let go of other thoughts and distractions. You can then ask further questions based on the answers they give you. For example, if you ask somebody where he lives, some follow-up questions might be "Why did your family move there?" "How do they like it there?" "How long have they lived there?" "What is there to do there?" and so on. As long as you can ask questions, you never have to worry about what to say in new situations. It can also be a lot of fun to investigate people and find out new things about them.

When you first meet people you can say things like "Nice to meet you," "Hi, how's it going," "Hello, my name is ____," or simply "Hi." When you start using the Sherlock Holmes, ask people questions about any topic at all. Here are some examples of questions and topics.

Some Introductory Questions

Where are you from? Where were you born?

How do you like it where you live? What's it like there?

How many people are there in your family?

What school do you go to? How do you like it there? How many kids are in your school?

What do you like to do for fun?

What's your favorite type of music?

What sports do you like? What's your favorite team?

Do you like to read? What kinds of books?

Do you ever go hiking or camping? Where have you gone?

What's your favorite type of food?

Where did your ancestors come from? Do you have relatives in this area?

Great Follow-Up Questions

What do you think about . . . ?

What's your opinion about . . . ?

Why do you think . . . ?

How do you feel about . . . ?

And then there are really fun, creative questions you can use with people once you get to know them a little better, like these.

Other Fun Questions

If you could be anybody else for a day, who would you want to be?

What's the bravest thing you've ever done?

Where would you most like to go on a vacation?

What's your absolute favorite main dish and dessert?

If you had $1 million that you had to spend in one day, how would you spend it?

If you could be like Johnny Appleseed, what trees would you want to plant everywhere?

If you could be any pro athlete for a day, who would you be?

What are your top three favorite movies?

If you could be any type of animal for a day, what would you be?

Once you get started, there's no limit to the questions you can ask, and people usually enjoy answering fun questions.

Practicing the Sherlock Holmes Together

You practice the Sherlock Holmes by having sit-down conversations with your child. Have your child initiate and maintain the dialogue. Also have him practice initial greetings with you.

Just have your child ask you questions. Make sure he or she listens to how you respond and asks follow-up questions. Your child can either ask you real questions or pretend that you're a new acquaintance and ask pretend questions. Even my teenage son has gotten a kick out of having for-fun "new acquaintance" conversation practices with his mother. You'll need to coach your child to pay explicit attention to the information you provide. Help him or her see how to use that information to ask even more questions.

Strive to include and engage your children in conversations when others are around. This needs to be done carefully by asking good inclusive questions ("Do you like *Star Wars,* too, Jenny?") not by badgering your kids or embarrassing them.

Technique 15: True Confessions

By itself the Sherlock Holmes is a very helpful tool for dealing with social conversational situations, but it's even more effective when complemented by True Confessions. Whereas the Sherlock Holmes involves asking questions and listening, True Confessions involves sympathizing and relating with others by confessing to our own thoughts, feelings, opinions, experiences, and foibles. It's opening up to people. When we disclose such information—how we feel and think about the object of conversation—social communication becomes a two-way flow, making others more comfortable about expressing themselves. People are more open with us when we're more open with them. True Confessions is an extension of the Power I. It's telling people how we feel and think in the context of friendly conversation.

True Confessions also involves expressing our feelings for others and the positive things they do in our lives. Boys and men sometimes have a hard time expressing how they feel. We need to define true masculine assertiveness for our boys as including expressing feelings toward others. Being able to honestly express things like "I really like you," "I really appreciate your help," "I like how I feel when I'm around you," and so forth is as important and assertive as any other type of expression.

Script to Introduce True Confessions

Another way to start and keep friendly conversations going with people is to tell them about yourself. People feel more comfortable about telling you about themselves if they see that you're willing to tell something about yourself. True Confessions means that you tell people about yourself at the same time that you're asking them questions. It means telling them about your own personal thoughts, feelings, and experiences. It includes telling them what you like about them and the things they enjoy—giving them compliments. True Confessions is just like the Power I but used in friendly conversation situations. Once again, you should never feel like you have to tell people about yourself, or to have conversations at all, but when you want to, True Confessions can help.

True Confessions can be used both when you first start up conversations and to keep them going. Here are some examples:

Starting Conversations with True Confessions

I've never read that book. Is it good?

I don't really like this music that much. How about you?

This homework is super hard for me. Do you mind if I ask you a couple of questions?

I always feel kind of shy in these situations. How about you?

I really liked watching the Olympics. Did you like them?

That's a neat bike. Where'd you get it?

Wow, you really know how to jump on the trampoline. Where'd you learn?

You've got a lot of cool baseball cards. Which are your favorites?

Responding to What the Other Person Says With True Confessions

Yeah, I don't like baseball either. How about basketball?

That's neat that you grew up in Kennebunkport. I would love it there.

I wish I could go to Hawaii like that. Were you there very long?

You were super brave. I'd probably feel chicken if I had to do that.

I would feel really bad if that happened to me, too.

I agree. I think it would be hard to run that far. How did you feel when you finished?

Remember that a very important part of True Confessions is to tell people honestly how you feel about them when you have good feelings toward them. Just like with other feelings, if we don't tell people who are special to us how we feel toward them, they may never know.

Some examples would be saying things like:

I really like how you are.

I really appreciate all the nice things you do for me.

I like how you share things with me.

I like it when you play with me.

I feel lucky to have a good friend like you.

We all feel really good when people who we like tell us things they like about us. Remember to use True Confessions to tell people what you like about them.

Practicing True Confessions Together

True Confessions is practiced in the same manner as the Sherlock Holmes. Ask your child to initiate a conversation with you by both asking questions (Sherlock Holmes) and by disclosing his or her own thoughts and feelings (True Confessions). As you practice, you may need to gently prompt your child to keep disclosing things. "Roger, what other things could you say about your own feelings and experiences?" "How could you help the other person to know that you understand?"

Teach your children about empathy by giving it to them. Let them know that you really remember how hard it can be sometimes to be a kid. Give them examples of your own experiences.

The absolute best way to teach your children to express their good feelings for others is to express your love and appreciation to them, other family members, friends, and others in direct, open ways.

Technique 16: Kind Talk

Sometimes in traditional assertiveness training programs, politeness is regarded as a weak and unnecessary vestige of former, unassertive times. But at the root of politeness is respect and civility. It's a matter of treating others as we would like to be treated. Nobody—neither child nor adult—likes to be ordered or bossed around. In a democratic society we seek the cooperation of people, not their servitude. Too often in our democracy we allow people to get away with dictatorial conduct. We allow ourselves to be treated in nonadult ways. If we're not spoken to with respectful words at home, at work, or in other situations, we have to use the Power I and teach people how we need to be treated. We need to have a mutual understanding with our children that we speak to each other with respect. If we want respect, we need to give it.

It's unfortunate that kindness in speech is sometimes viewed as a sign of weakness or being a goody-goody. Cultures that ridicule kindness and elevate crudeness and offensiveness reap the fruits of that orientation. Life in such cultures is less enjoyable.

Kind Talk not only means actively using the words "please" and "thank you" but also means refraining from using mean and cruel words with others. It means treating others with verbal respect. Using "please" and "thank you" is a good starting point, but it needs to extend to avoiding cruelty in speech. As much as possible, without being overbearing about it, my wife and I try to encourage Kind Talk in our home. Our frequent parental refrain is "Kind Talk, please."

Part of Kind Talk is also learning to respond to compliments children receive from others. Sometimes children simply don't know how to respond to compliments. They feel awkward and uncomfortable. It's important that they learn to say "thank you" in ways that are comfortable for them when they receive compliments.

As with all techniques, but especially with this one, it's vital that parents teach through example. It's especially important that you use Kind Talk with your children.

Script to Introduce Kind Talk

It's very good to treat people in the same way we'd like to be treated. The world would be an even greater place if we all tried to live like that. One way we can do that is in talking to others. Kind Talk means that we use the words "please" and "thank you" when we talk to other people. Nobody likes to be bossed around. When we use the word "please" we're showing that we don't consider people our servants, we consider them our equals and worthy of our respect. Likewise, "thank you" shows our respect and gratitude when others help us. While it's true that we're as good as anybody else, we're no better.

Kind Talk also means that we don't talk to people in a really mean way. We talk to them as we would want them to talk to us. Sometimes we need to speak to people in a strong and angry voice to stop them from doing harmful things or things we just don't like. But otherwise it's good to speak to people respectfully. We'll call for Kind Talk whenever we hear too much mean talk going on. We expect you to speak to us with respect, and we also need to speak to you with respect. If we forget, remind us.

We can also use Kind Talk when people give us a compliment. We simply thank people for the compliment, just like we would thank them for any other kind thing they might do for us. Sometimes it's hard to just say good old "Thanks!" when people give us a compliment—it might feel like we're bragging a little bit to agree with them, even though we're really not. When it feels this way, it might help to compliment them back when we thank them, by saying things like "Thanks, that's nice of you to say" or "Well, thank you, that's really kind" or "Thanks for noticing."

Practicing Kind Talk Together

If your children don't habitually use Kind Talk, it may be important to take them aside from time to time and give them kind reminders. When they don't use Kind Talk with you directly, you can simply express to them directly how you want them to talk to you (using the Power I; see Chapter 1).

You can also do role playing.

Role-Playing Examples

Feel free to substitute your own age-relevant wording.

Parent: First, let's practice "please."

Let's say you want me to pick you up from school.

Child: Could you please pick me up from school?

Parent: Let's say you want somebody to help you with a homework problem.

Child: Could you please help me with this problem?

Parent: Let's say you want me to pass you some bread.

Child: Could you please pass me the bread?

Parent: Now, let's practice "thank you."

Let's say somebody picks up a book you drop and gives it to you.

Child: Thanks.

Parent: Let's say somebody helps you with the homework problem.

Child: Thanks.

Parent: Let's say I get something for you from the refrigerator.

Child: Thanks.

Parent: Let's say our neighbor gives you a ride home from school.

Child: Thanks a lot for the ride.

Parent: Let's also practice using "thank you" when somebody gives you a compliment, which means she tells you that she likes something about you. I'll give you a compliment, and you respond with some version of "thanks."

I really like the way you helped me do the dishes.

Child: Thanks.

Parent: That shirt looks really good on you.

Child: Thanks.

Parent: Boy, you really know how to play baseball.

Child: Thanks.

Parent: Finally, I'm going to give you some examples of unkind words, and I want you to tell me how those words could be changed using Kind Talk: How could you make this statement not so mean: "Go get my book for me right now!"?

Child: "When you're up, could you please get my book?"

Parent: How could you make this statement not so mean: "You're so lazy, you little creep, get up and get your own book."

Child: "I can't do that right now—you're going to have to get your book yourself."

Parent: How could your make this statement not so mean: "I'm starving. You said you'd get something to eat. I need something to eat right now!"?

Child: "I'm really hungry. Could you please help me get some food?"

Parent: How could you make this statement not so mean: "You're such a big baby! All I do is ask you to help me and you can't do anything but sit there"?

Child: "I really need your help. How can I get you to help?"

Parent: How could you make this statement not so mean: "You never play games with me. You never think of anybody but yourself. You're so selfish. I hate you"?

Child: "I feel bad when you won't play with me. When can you play with me?"

Parent: How could you make this statement not so mean: "You were supposed to wash my pants. Where are they? Didn't you do the laundry?"?

Child: "Did you have a chance to wash my pants? I need to have them for school tomorrow."

CHAPTER SIX

The Way of the Owl: Responding to Self-defeating Thoughts

Owls are symbols of wisdom and perspective. They are both observant and perceptive. Like other birds of prey, they sit in calm focus waiting for their prey. But, unlike other birds of prey, they also have the ability to see and hear extraordinarily well in the dark. The Way of the Owl is the way of seeing clearly in the dark, the way of gaining perspective when we feel helpless or unhappy.

When our daughter was three, we brought home a family dog. We were unpleasantly surprised to find that Brooke was terrified of him. She couldn't be within eyesight of the dog without becoming overwhelmed by intense fear. So after a few weeks, we prepared to take the dog back. Then, in a single day, we were amazed to find that her view of the dog had completely changed. Suddenly, after those fearful weeks, she was holding the dog and playing with him. She's experienced this type of breakthrough thinking in other areas of her life. She changes how she thinks about something, and soon she's dealing with it very comfortably. We need to remind our children that negative thoughts aren't forever; they have the power to change them.

The verbal techniques discussed so far are for responding to the words of other people. But perhaps the most critically important techniques are those that help children respond to the words they say to themselves—to their own automatic thoughts and beliefs. A great deal of our children's happiness is dependent on what they believe about themselves and how they explain the events of life to themselves—whether they have an optimistic or pessimistic explanatory style.

Over the past few decades, cognitive therapists have confirmed the strong connection between thoughts and feelings. Our feelings come from our thoughts. If our thoughts are habitually unreasonable and pessimistic, we will feel a great deal of helplessness and unhappiness.

Very young children are often optimistic. But as they grow older, they develop their core beliefs about themselves and about life. If their core beliefs about themselves are generally pessimistic and rigid, the seeds are sown for helplessness and unhappiness.

As Dr. Martin Seligman contends in his book *Learned Optimism,* optimism isn't the power of positive thinking, it's the power of "non-negative" thinking. It's changing the self-defeating, destructive words we sometimes say to ourselves.

As parents we have a wonderful opportunity to help our children develop beliefs and thinking habits that can help them to be happy and beneficial adults. Next to love, this is the most important legacy we can give our children.

An optimistic explanatory style explains setbacks and bad events as temporary, isolated, external (not personalized), and irrelevant to the basic worth of the person involved. A pessimistic style explains setbacks and bad events as permanent ("it's going to last forever"), pervasive ("it's going to ruin everything"), and very personal ("it's all my fault"). Research strongly suggests that children learn their optimistic or pessimistic explanatory thinking habits from their primary caregivers: from the explanatory models that the caregivers provide, from how the children are criticized, and from how they're helped to gain perspective when they go through traumatic events.

The really good thing is that it's never too late to influence our children's beliefs and how they respond to pessimistic thoughts.As parents we have a wonderful opportunity to help our children develop beliefs and thinking habits that can make it easier for them to be happy and beneficial adults. We can reconfirm their permanent, abiding worth, and we can help them understand that life's difficult events are normal, temporary, and not to be taken too personally. Next to love, this is the most important legacy we can leave our children.

Children first need to be taught that their feelings come from their thoughts. Feelings of helplessness and unhappiness come directly from the thoughts they are reviewing and believing. These thoughts can be so quick and automatic that it's sometimes hard even to notice them.

Second, they need to respond to the self-defeating thoughts that are causing their feelings. This is done by disputing the thoughts—by not letting pessimistic, unreasonable thoughts just slip by. Children need to know that we create some of our thoughts and we can change them.

In the case of helplessness, our kids also need to learn how to come up with practical solutions and get things done. (I'll discuss problem-solving techniques later in this chapter.) Reaffirming their worth and refraining from overcorrecting our children doesn't mean that we don't encourage them to work hard and not give up. On the contrary, for their long-term resilience and general well-being, our kids need to learn to finish difficult tasks successfully. In Chapter 7 I'll introduce the Mindful Chores practice as one method of helping this along.

As I've said, it's essential that our children understand another fundamental principle—that they are not their thoughts. In the same way the words that others tell them are not them, the words that they tell themselves, or that automatically come to them, are not them—your children simply are. It's only natural that a wide variety of thoughts and feelings should come to us—this is part of being a human being. It's instructive from time to time to simply sit by the "stream" of our thoughts and feelings and take note of what's going on in a nonjudgmental manner. It's helpful to view our thoughts and feelings as sensations and events. But the reality is that we are not our thoughts and feelings—we simply are.

The techniques involved in the Way of the Owl require that children first learn to become aware of their feelings and the thoughts associated with them. They then learn, with our help, to respond to self-defeating thoughts with reaffirming, optimistic thoughts. They also learn to deal with real-life problems by developing and implementing solutions. The ultimate goal is to help our children have core beliefs that tell them, "I'm worthwhile," "I can," and "Things aren't so bad."

The techniques in the Way of the Owl are based on the work of authorities in cognitive therapy. In addition to the works of Martin Seligman, I recommend a popular trade book entitled *Feeling Good* by Dr. David Burns for an overview of this therapy. There's a strong linkage between cognitive therapy and mindfulness. Cognitive therapy is essentially paying attention in the present moment, in a nonjudgmental way, to bothersome thoughts and feelings that flow through us, then responding to those thoughts in constructive ways.

SCRIPT TO INTRODUCE THE WAY OF THE OWL

Owls are symbols for wisdom. One of the neat things about owls is that they can see really well in the dark. Sometimes we have feelings that seem kind of dark because they make us feel bad inside. These feelings can keep us from doing things we need to get done and from being happy. The Way of the Owl is learning how to change the way we think about things, so we can change unhappy feelings that get in our way.

Technique 17: But Twist

Besides being a term that my children love to say, the But Twist is a very simple first line of defense against feelings of helplessness. The greatest impediment to children doing things they need to do usually isn't the difficulty of the task—it's usually an "I can't" thought: "It's too hard," "I don't feel like it," "I just can't do it," "I feel lazy." The But Twist is an internal verbal technique that kids use to respond to these types of thoughts. Rather than letting "I can't" thoughts win the day, the But Twist helps turn these thoughts around. This is done simply by adding the word "but" at the end of such thoughts and providing a reason for taking the desired action anyway. For example, if a child has a chore to do, such as mowing the lawn, and a thought comes to her like "I just don't feel like it," the But Twist response might be, "*But* the sooner I do it, the quicker it'll be over" or "*But* it really isn't that hard once I get started" or "*But* I'll just walk out to the garage as a start and take it from there."

Parents can be very helpful by occasionally brainstorming with children to identify possible But Twist phrases in specific situations. The But Twist directly triggers the replacement of "I can't" thoughts with "but I can" thoughts.

Sometimes there's need for a "tough love" version of the But Twist. Kids can be so overwhelmed by whiny thinking that they can't gain perspective without some help. You can give them a choice between doing the thing that needs to be done and doing something much harder, as in, "You can either do the dishes right now, or you can do both the dishes and vacuum the house" or "You can do this twenty minutes' worth of homework right now, or else you can do both the homework and pull weeds in the yard." This approach provides your kids with an automatic, ready-made But Twist: "It's not fun to do my homework right now, *but* it's better than doing both my homework and pulling weeds."

In addition to using the But Twist, children can learn to overcome "I can't" thinking by practicing doing things with less emotional upheaval. In Chapter 7 there are two mindfulness practices, the Rock and Mindful Chores, that can be used to teach kids how to do things more effortlessly.

Sometimes we also simply need to push our children to do hard things, not unlike the way a mother bird must push her fledglings to fly. Our children's ultimate resilience depends on being able to do hard things. But our pushing needs to be done in a way that preserves their self-regard. In the history of men's NCAA basketball, there's never been a more successful coach than John

Wooden. His teams at UCLA won an astounding ten national championships. Amazingly, Wooden never pushed "winning." He pushed his players to work hard, achieve peak performance, and be prepared. But he didn't explicitly push winning. He pushed his players without berating them. He gave them positive encouragement and treated them with dignity and respect. His teams had a calm confidence and a high level of self-regard. Coaches and parents can learn from Wooden's example—it's good to prod our children to work hard, as long as it's done with words of encouragement and respect. Sometimes this requires our own versions of the Power I, the Squeaky Wheel, Solution Time, and, of course, Kind Talk.

This doesn't mean that we have to put our children in highly competitive situations. If they're not particularly talented, these situations can be destructive, since they can foster the development of false beliefs of general inadequacy and inferiority. Trying hard and working hard don't ever need to be framed in terms of competitive sports, for example—there are many good outlets for developing determination, competency, and a sense of success. These outlets can be anything from doing chores, raising a pet, and excelling in a class at school to pursuing music, art, drama or public volunteer activities.

Script to Introduce the But Twist

Sometimes there are things in life that we have to get done. We have to do them because our family, teachers at school, or people in need require them. Or we have to do them because they can get us something we really want—like earning money for college, becoming a really good athlete, or getting good grades. Some of those things take some real effort, and they're not always fun. It's only natural in those situations to have thoughts that tell us it's too hard and we can't do it. These are "I can't" thoughts. These thoughts can make things seem harder than they really are. One of the best ways to still get things done with "I can't" thoughts is to talk back to them.

The But Twist is a technique for talking back to "I can't" thoughts. When you notice that an "I can't" thought comes to you, you use the word "but" and then make new thoughts that help you do what needs to be done anyway. For example, if you need to do some homework and a thought comes that says, "I just don't feel like it," you could respond with *"But* I can just sit down and start for a few minutes and see how it goes" or *"But* if I just get it done, it'll be really nice to have it all over with" or *"But* it's never that hard once I get started.

Remember that in real life I sometimes need to push you to get things done. This is part of my job as a parent.

If a task is dangerous or harmful, pay attention to your "I can't" thought and don't do it. Here are some examples of common But Twists that can help:

But I can do it.

But it's really not that hard.

But it really won't take very long.

But I can just take one small step at a time.

But it'll be great to have it done.

But it won't kill me.

But I'm just having a feeling about it—I'll jump in and see how hard it really is.

But I can just start and see how it goes.

But I can ask for help if it gets too hard.

I'm going to pretend that I'm some "I can't" thoughts that come into your mind, and I want you to respond to these thoughts with a couple of examples of the But Twist.

Practicing the But Twist Together:
Role-Playing Examples
Feel free to substitute your own age-relevant wording.

Parent: You need to do your homework, and a thought comes that says, "This is too hard, I can't do it." Give me two examples of possible But Twists.

Child: "But the sooner I get started, the less I'll have to do tomorrow" or "But I can at least try it, and if it really becomes painful, I can get Mom to help."

Parent: You've been asked to wash the dishes, and a thought comes that says, "I don't want to, I'm just not in the mood." Give me two examples of possible But Twists.

Child: "But it really isn't hard once I get started" or "But I'll feel great once it's finished and I don't have to think about it."

Parent: You have to run a mile in PE and a thought

comes to you that says, "I can't do this." Give me two examples of possible But Twists.

Child: "But I can just take it slow and see what happens" or "But it won't kill me."

Parent: You need to practice the piano and the thought comes, "I just don't feel like it." Give me two examples of But Twists.

Child: "But I just need to take one little note at a time" or "But if I keep practicing a little bit every day, some day I'll be able to play really well."

Parent: You need to go out in the snow and help a neighbor shovel his sidewalk when it's really cold and the thought comes, "It's too cold, I just can't do it." Give me two examples of But Twists.

Child: "But I'll just put on a lot of extra clothes" or "But it'll really help my neighbor—it won't take all that long."

In everyday life, as children say they can't do things that you've maturely determined really need to get done, help them come up with But Twists that they can use for those situations.

Remember, though, that sometimes enough is enough. Whiny thinking may overwhelm our children's thoughts, and they may need the "tough love" version of the But Twist. They can't gain perspective without your help. As described earlier, you offer this by giving them the choice between doing the thing that needs to be done and doing something much harder. This provides them with a ready-made But Twist—as in "This isn't fun, but it could be a lot worse."

Use the Rock and Mindful Chores practices described in Chapter 7 to help your children practice doing things with less anguish and turmoil.

Technique 18: Solution Time 2 (for Solving Problems)

The But Twist is a good first step for dealing with thoughts and feelings of helplessness. But if there are real-life problems behind our helpless feelings, there is probably nothing more empowering than to develop and implement solutions to those problems. A solution-oriented approach to life can help children develop a greater sense of self-efficacy—a key element in personal resilience, according to Dr. Albert Bandura of Stanford University. We've already learned to use Solution Time as a tool to resolve conflicts. Solution Time can also be used as a general problem-solving tool. As discussed in Chapter 4, Solution Time is a time-out used for coming up with ideas to solve problems. By seeing problems as puzzles to be solved, as opposed to burdens or evidence of self-limitations, children can feel empowered by their ability to deal with problem situations.

The first step is to begin to get in a Solution Time mode as problems arise. The problems can range from anything like challenges with schoolwork to difficulty with other kids in the neighborhood. As children get older their problems may become more serious, like how to deal with a fledgling drinking or drug problem or what to do with the rest of their lives. But, depending upon how they view the world, any stage of life can appear traumatic for children who haven't learned to solve problems.

You can initiate Solution Time whenever you recognize that your children have problems that need to be solved. The key is to get your children to spend more energy on creating solutions (planning on how to get what they really need) and less energy on creating and churning over problems (focusing on what they can't do and don't have). Generating solutions takes mental exertion. Like any other skill that involves exertion, it requires practice. You shouldn't step in and solve the problems directly for your children but rather act as a mentor in teaching them the steps of generating and implementing solutions. Most successful approaches to solving problems include at least the following steps:

1. Figure out what really needs to be accomplished—the purpose involved.
2. Generate solution options.
3. Weigh the advantages and disadvantages of each option—including likely consequences (and do more investigation if necessary).
4. Select an option and implement it.

This process can sometimes be helped along by using a solution rating table. First of all, confirm what needs to be accomplished. In the far-left column, write out the key factors to be used in rating the solutions. Across the top row, write out all the solution ideas your child and you come up with. For each combination of key factors and solutions (cells), rank all the solutions.

As an example, let's say your child needs to get a grade of B or higher in a difficult math class. Below is a table of possible key factors and solutions. The solution that best deals with the factor receives a 1, the second best receives a 2 and so on.

Purpose: To get a grade of B or higher in math class

Solution Options

Key Factors	Get More Help from Teacher	Hire a Tutor	Stricter Homework Schedule	More Parent Tutoring
Most likely successful method	3 (tie)	2	3 (tie)	1
Most showing of parental interest and support	3	3	2	1
Least required extra child time	1	3 (tie)	2	3 (tie)
Least required extra parent time	1	2	3	4
Least money cost	1 (tie)	2	1 (tie)	1 (tie)

The solution option "More Parent Tutoring" dominates with three important factors, and "Get More Help from Teacher" is also dominant (although with three factors that probably aren't as critical, unless the parent is really strapped for time). Using a rating table, especially for more complicated problems, can narrow down the choices. If more than one dominant option remains, you can then make tradeoffs (based on how you weigh the importance of the factors) or decide how the details of an option could be modified to make it even more dominant and clear-cut. In the above example, if the parent can find a way to tutor in a very time-efficient manner (through the use of computer tutoring tools, for example), the last option might become even more dominant. See the book *Smart Choices: A Practical Guide to Making Better Decisions* (by John S. Hammond, Ralph L. Keeney, and Howard Raiffa, published by Harvard Business School in 1998) for further examples of solution rating tables and other problem-solving tools.

When your child has problems that are causing helplessness or difficulty, call for a Solution Time. This is a time for you to slow down and to put aside the urgency of your own matters and focus on helping your child develop concrete solutions to real-life problems and worries.

Solution Time is also a great venue for dealing with behavioral problems and establishing house rules. The time can be used to mutually determine rules and consequences (if the rules aren't kept). Just make sure to stick to the agreed-to plan.

Script to Introduce Solution Time for Solving Problems

Sometimes we have bad feelings and tough times because there are real problems to solve or tough choices to make. We've already discussed Solution Time as a way to deal with conflicts and fights. Now we're going to talk about Solution Time as a tool for solving other kinds of problems.

You always need to feel free to come to me for help with your problems. What we'll do is sit down together and have a Solution Time. This will involve the following:

1. *Decide what the real problem is.* For example, if you're having a problem with a class in school, we'll try to figure out what your real purpose or objective is. Would it be to really understand the subject, to get interested in the subject, to make sure you can at least pass the tests, or to get a B or better?

2. *Come up with solution ideas.* We'll make a list if we need to. For example, if your real purpose is to get a B or better in the class, we might list things like go talk to the teacher together to see what needs to be done, hire a tutor, set up a schedule for homework, have me spend more time with you, get learning materials that are easier to understand, and so forth.

3. *Look at the strong points and weak points* of each solution idea and choose one. We'll try to figure out what each solution requires and the types of things (both good and bad) that might happen if we choose it. If we're looking at a difficult problem, we might have to do further investigation (either talk to other people or

do research in the library or on the Internet). We'll figure out what tasks we need to carry out to gather further information.

4. Once we've settled on a solution, we'll *decide how to get the solution done.* We might even need to list the necessary tasks and set deadlines for each one.

When I see problems that need to be dealt with, I'm going to start calling for a Solution Time.

Practicing Solution Time Together

Solution Time is taught through real-life experience and mentoring. Children should be reminded that whenever they have a problem that is upsetting to them, they should come and tell you so you can do Solution Time together.

Call for Solution Time whenever problems arise that clearly need to be dealt with. Put pen to paper to list solutions together. This can be done when children raise problems that they haven't been willing to deal with, including the common "I'm bored" refrain. Prod them to create their own solutions.

Technique 19: Thought Chop

Sometimes in the martial arts a person needs to strongly counter an offensive assault. The Thought Chop is meant to provide a verbal counterblow to unreasonable internal words that bring us unhappiness. As mentioned previously, we want our children to do good and to be happy. "I can't" thoughts get in the way of our children doing good, and "I'm bad" or "things are terrible" thoughts get in the way of them being happy. The But Twist and Solution Time are tools that are especially helpful for responding to "I can't" situations. The Thought Chop will help kids respond to the types of "I'm bad" and "things are terrible" thoughts that come up when difficult things happen to them.

The first step in helping our children deal with self-defeating thinking is to encourage them to notice their feelings and to feel comfortable talking about them. Depending on the ages of the children, we can talk to them about noticing their "happy" or "positive" feelings on the one hand, and their "sad" or "negative" feelings on the other. It's important that children begin to understand that their feelings are not "them" or "reality" but are simply feelings. In fact, our feelings are a very helpful internal thinking "thermometer." They are an automatic feedback mechanism to let us know if our beliefs and habits of thought are healthy or self-defeating. If we feel bad too often, too easily, or for too long, we know that we need to change our beliefs and thinking habits.

The second step is to help our children notice the thoughts that are producing their feelings. These thoughts can be based on false beliefs that they've adopted about themselves and the world. They can also be based on pessimistic thinking habits they've developed to explain life's events. These habits center on thinking in exaggerated, simplistic ways—ways that view bad events as permanent, pervasive, and personalized. Some events in life, like death, serious illness, and dire poverty, *are* truly terrible. Constructive explanatory styles don't deny the reality of difficult events. They just make sure that our thoughts don't affect our internal lives well beyond the meaning of the events themselves. Our thoughts can make many everyday events seem much worse and pervasive than they are.

The third step is to help our children dispute their self-defeating thoughts. They need to counter false beliefs with correct ones. They also need to begin to see difficult events as temporary bumps in the road that happen to everyone, not as permanent evidence of personal failure. I'm always excited as a basketball coach when I see players who miss a shot or lose the ball, then just hustle back into position without a care in the world. I know that such players have a healthy perspective on both the game and life. Looser players play better in the clutch. The But Twist is a good tool to dispute "I can't" thoughts. The Thought Chop helps kids talk back to self-defeating false beliefs and thinking mistakes that can lead to "I'm bad" and "things are terrible" thoughts.

As an independently minded school board member, I believe that some advocates and educators involved in the "self-esteem" movement are off course. Like Coach John Wooden, I'm not big on grades ("winning"), but I am big on preparation and effort, and then letting the grades ("winning") take care of themselves. Kids don't develop self-esteem by avoiding all difficult tasks and possible setbacks. On the contrary, competence and resilience, which are developed through real effort and coping with setbacks, are vital elements of self-esteem. We do nothing to help our children by eliminating all rigor from education (which isn't the same thing as dish-ing out a lot of homework). Rather than eliminate all difficulty, we need to ensure that we eliminate negative criticism of our children when they do have setbacks, give them support and personalized help, increase our encouragement, and help them get back on their feet when they take a tumble. But they need lots of practice at trying, having some setbacks, and experiencing success—just like when they first learned to ride a bicycle. When it comes to building self-esteem, more important than pointing out every special and positive thing about our children (and risking narcissism), we need to just be especially vigilant about avoiding negative criticism. "That's okay, just keep at it" is what our kids need to hear.

Research tells us that the model we provide for our children in explaining life's events is critical. We need to examine how we respond to life's events when we're around our children. We need to learn not to overreact to life's ups and downs. It's also important to examine our own basic beliefs and thinking habits, since we naturally pass along our beliefs and attitudes to our children. Our beliefs and attitudes form the culture of our home life.

As humans, we frequently achieve adulthood physically and mentally before we do so emotionally. Maturing emotionally requires adopting new adult-level beliefs and perspective. Without this transformation, adults can be emotionally imprisoned by self-defeating beliefs that they have held since childhood or adolescence. We all have examples in our lives where we have changed our beliefs. Many of us spend years in college or in the workplace evaluating and adopting knowledge that is different from our childhood understanding of things. Yet we sometimes spend no time at all evaluating some of our most fundamental, self-defeating beliefs about ourselves and the world that we've been holding on to since childhood. Why not evaluate and change the false childhood beliefs that bring us unhappiness?

Given our unique backgrounds, it's only natural that we have the thoughts and feelings we currently have. But it's also within our natural power to change the thoughts, beliefs, and actions that promote unhappiness. I'll discuss some of the major categories of self-defeating beliefs and thinking errors in detail in the following script. The script is divided into two parts, False Beliefs and Thinking Mistakes. I've found it helpful to review this material with kids in two or more sittings, since there's a lot to absorb and it can take kids some effort to achieve this perspective.

Script to Introduce the Thought Chop

Feelings are a wonderful thing. Can you imagine what life would be like if we didn't have feelings? Without feelings we'd be like robots. We wouldn't want to play games, go on hikes, be with our family, tell jokes, help each other, or do many of the things we need and want to do. We wouldn't know happiness, love, kindness, peace, excitement, fun, or sympathy without our feelings. Feelings are like sugar and salt—they give life all its flavor.

Sometimes we have feelings that feel bad. These might be fear, guilt, worry, anger, and sadness. Part of being human is to have these feelings, and sometimes they can help us. Fear can help us run fast when we're in danger. Worry can help us prepare for important future events. Anger can give us the courage to stop somebody from doing something harmful. Guilt can help us stop ourselves from doing something harmful. Sadness can help us heal when we've gone through a painful experience. But sometimes our thoughts make it so that we have these feelings too often or for too long, even when we don't need them.

There are two very important things to remember about our feelings:

1. Our feelings come from our thoughts. In order to change feelings, we first need to change our thoughts.
2. We are not our feelings, we simply are. Like a stream of water, our thoughts and feelings flow through us, but they aren't us. No matter how you feel, your thoughts and feelings aren't you.

The first step in changing feelings that we don't want is to notice them. Do you have bad feelings very often? In what kinds of situations? Whenever you have these feelings and you're bothered by them, you should let me know so that we can talk about them. You need to feel free to honestly express your feelings to me at any time.

The second step is to notice the thoughts that are causing our feelings. Thoughts that say to us things like "I'm bad" or "things are terrible" are the types of thoughts that can make us feel worse than we need to. A lot of times these thoughts come from false beliefs or thinking mistakes.

The final step is to figure out some words to use to talk back to your thoughts. We've already learned how to do this with the But Twist, where you came up with words to talk back to "I can't" thoughts. A technique called the Thought Chop is used to talk back to "I'm bad" or "things are terrible" thoughts. The Thought Chop can help us feel better and tougher when hard things happen.

Let's first review some common false beliefs and thinking mistakes. Then we'll practice the Thought Chop together.

FALSE BELIEFS

Our beliefs are our opinions about ourselves and the world. An example of a false belief is that dogs can fly, or that the moon is made of cheese, or that the earth is flat [give your kids examples of false beliefs in history]. We can change beliefs that aren't true. Did you have any funny beliefs when you were really little?

One of the most important beliefs that can make us feel happy or unhappy is our belief about ourselves. You always need to remember that any belief that makes you feel you're not good is a false belief. As a creation of God, you're as good as anybody or anything else on the planet. This doesn't mean that you'll always *do* good. You need to do something kind and helpful to *do* good. But you don't need to do anything at all to *be* good—you were born that way. You're a wonderful, normal human being with natural strengths and weaknesses.

Let's talk about four very common false beliefs:

1. *It's bad if somebody doesn't like you.* Mountains and trees don't need to be liked, and neither do you. You're at least as good as a mountain or tree or anything else on the planet. Part of life is to be disliked by other people. Many great people in history have been disliked by a lot of people. People like Abraham Lincoln, Martin Luther King, and Eleanor Roosevelt were disliked by people when they were alive. It's only natural that for every person who likes you, there might be another one who doesn't. Being liked has nothing to do with your goodness.

Have you ever had this belief come to you? Here are some Thought Chops you can use for this type of false belief:

- Some people like you and some people don't, that's just the way life is.
- I don't want to be liked if it means doing and saying what others want me to all the time.
- Sometimes it's good to disagree with people and not be liked.
- I'm just as good as anybody else, no matter who likes me.
- If people don't like me, that's their problem.

2. *You're bad if you make mistakes.* Mistakes are a natural part of life. Part of being human is to have accidents and make mistakes. You can't be on this planet without them. Just as our thoughts and feelings are not us, our accidents and mistakes are not us. Our family expects you not to do harmful things on purpose. We expect you to make up for harmful mistakes and not do them again. But it's false to think that you're not good if you make mistakes.

Have you ever had this belief come to you? Here are some Thought Chops you can use for this type of false belief:

- It's normal to sometimes make mistakes and have accidents.
- Everybody makes mistakes.
- Bad things happen to everybody.
- These things happen.
- I'll try better next time.

3. *You've done a bad job if you haven't done your best.* Sometimes to accomplish important things, we've got to go all out and do our best. But we all have bad days. And many times it's okay to do just okay. In fact, it's usually better to do just okay on unimportant things, so that we can spend more time and effort on the things that really matter. It's good always to try

and not give up when things need to get done. But many times good enough is good enough. Just getting things done can be a great accomplishment.

Have you ever had this belief come to you? Here are some Thought Chops you can use for this type of false belief:

- It's normal not to do everything perfectly.
- Everybody has bad days.
- Good enough is good enough.
- Just to finish things that need to get done is great.
- A lot of life is just patching the biggest leak in the roof.

4. *Things have to turn out the way you want or you can't be happy.* Many times we can't have exactly what we want. Life isn't always easy or fun. Bad things happen. But this doesn't mean we have to be unhappy in those situations. Many great people in history have had difficult lives. People like George Washington, Jackie Robinson, and Helen Keller were able to have successful, happy lives even though they had to go through a lot of hard things. Happy feelings come from our thoughts, not from what we have or don't have.

Have you ever had this belief come to you? Here are some Thought Chops you can use for this type of false belief:

- Life can't always be easy, but I can still be happy.
- It's normal to not always get what you want.
- Hard things happen to everyone.
- This will pass.
- What solution can I come up with to help me through this?

Remember that what's true of you is also true of others. Other people are also normal humans who have natural strengths and weaknesses. It's normal for others to sometimes make mistakes and not do things perfectly. We need to be patient with others.

Thinking Mistakes

Another thinking problem that can make us have bad feelings too easily is thinking mistakes. Thinking mistakes often come when hard things happen to us. Good and bad things happen to everybody. There are some events that are really terrible, like death, serious illness, and dire poverty. But our thinking mistakes can make everyday events seem a lot worse than they really are. I want to review with you six types of thinking mistakes.

1. *Exaggerating*

Exaggerating is thinking that something is worse than it really is. I'm going to give you some examples of this type of thinking, and you tell me the mistakes these thoughts are making:

- This apple doesn't taste good, so it's the worst apple in the world.
- I can't find anything to do, so our town is the most boring place in the world.
- The boy I like doesn't like me, so I can never be happy again.
- I didn't do well on the test, so I'm really stupid.

2. *Focusing on the Bad*

Focusing on the Bad is seeing only the bad parts of things, instead of all the parts, including the good parts. I'm going to give you some examples of this type of thinking, and you tell me the mistakes these thoughts are making:

- This apple has a scratch on it, so it's bad.
- Our town has crime, so it's bad.
- I don't do well in math, so I'm a bad student.
- The teacher made a negative comment on one page of my report, so it stinks.

3. *All-or-Nothing Thinking*

All-or-Nothing Thinking is when you see things as completely one way or the other. I'm going to give you some examples of this type of thinking, and you tell me the mistakes these thoughts are making:

- If I can't have all the apples in this bowl, it's not good to have any of them.
- If our town can't be 100 percent safe, it's not safe at all.
- I need to get an A in my math class or I've failed.
- If I don't make the team, I'm a total failure.

4. *Labeling*

Labeling is when you think that because one thing is bad, all similar things are bad. I'm going to give you some examples of this type of thinking, and you tell me the mistakes these thoughts are making:

- This apple is rotten, so all apples are rotten.
- That man is a robber, so everyone in his neighborhood is a robber.
- I had a bad game, so I'm a bad basketball player.
- I embarrassed myself trying out for the play, so I'm a jerk.

5. *Jumping to Conclusions*

Jumping to Conclusions is guessing that something will be bad without really knowing. I'm going to give you some examples of this type of thinking, and you tell me the mistakes these thoughts are making:

- This apple is funny looking, so it's going to have worms in it.
- Our new neighbors look unfriendly, so I know I won't like them.
- Mary's not going to be at the party, so I know I won't have any fun.
- My teacher yelled at me, so I'm going to get a lousy report card.

6. *Blaming Ourselves*

Blaming Ourselves is taking personal blame for things when we don't need to. I'm going to give you some examples of this type of thinking, and you tell me the mistakes these thoughts are making:

- A worm got in my apple, so it's my fault.
- Our neighborhood isn't as friendly as it could be, so it's my fault.
- I missed one goal in our soccer game, so it's my fault we lost.
- If I hadn't argued with my boyfriend, he wouldn't have dumped me.

These thinking mistakes often happen when we experience bad events. You always need to remember that bad events happen to everybody, they don't last forever, they don't have to affect the other good parts of your life, and you're as good as anybody else, even if bad things happen to you or if you make mistakes. Here are some examples of quick and simple Thought Chops that can help when hard things happen.

THOUGHT CHOPS

I'll get over it.

This is a normal part of life.

These things happen.

Everybody makes mistakes.

Some people like you and some don't.

What's the worst that can happen because of this?

I'll just pick myself up and keep trying.

I just had a bad day.

Nobody's perfect.

I tried, and it just didn't work out.

I'll be ready next time.

I'll just keep pushing.

It's no big deal.

It's not that bad.

This will pass.

I can't do it all.

Sometimes you win and sometimes you lose.

Tomorrow's a new day.

I'm just as good as anybody else.

I'm a normal human being with natural strengths and weaknesses.

I'll just sit down and have a Solution Time.

Note to Parents: Some would argue that if kids are too easy on themselves, they won't excel. Research, however, suggests the opposite. According to Martin Seligman, who has studied explanatory styles, the most successful athletes and sports teams tend to be the ones that have the most optimistic explanatory styles when things don't go well. Studies of pro baseball and basketball teams show that success in the game is predicted by optimism (above and beyond how "good" a team is). All other things being equal, teams with players who explain bad events to themselves as "It wasn't our day" or "The other team just played well" outperform teams with players who explain such events with "We just can't hit" or "We don't play with confidence." Clearly, kids sometimes need to go all out and try really hard. That's an issue of pushing them along when we need to. But they don't need to beat themselves up when things don't go well. On the contrary, they need to *keep* from beating themselves up. They'll have a much better chance of performing at peak levels if they can deal optimistically with setbacks. We want them to be able to pick themselves up from the ground and keep at it; we don't want them to lay on the ground wallowing in "I can't," "I'm bad," "this is terrible" thinking.

Practicing the Thought Chop Together:

Role-Playing Examples

Feel free to substitute your own age-relevant wording.

Parent: To practice the Thought Chop, I'm going to give you some hard situations, and I want you to give me a few Thought Chops that you could tell yourself in those situations.

You play in a soccer game as the goalie, and the other team makes a goal off you in the last few seconds to win the game, and a thought comes that says, "I lost the entire game." Give me a few Thought Chops.

Child: "That kid made a terrific kick," "Hey, that's part of the game," "Sometimes you win and sometimes you lose," "I'll get over it," "I made a great effort, it just slipped by," "That was one play out of about a hundred different plays in the game," "I'm not blaming anyone because they didn't make enough goals."

Parent: You like a boy at school and find out that he likes somebody else, and a thought comes that says, "I can't be happy if he doesn't like me." Give me a few Thought Chops.

Child: "I like him, but there are plenty of other boys," "I'll get over it," "Frankly, it's his loss," "People don't have to be liked to be happy," "Sometimes you win and sometimes you lose," "What's the worst that can happen if he doesn't like me?"

Parent: You run for president of your school and lose, and a thought comes that says, "I should have never run." Give me a few Thought Chops.

Child: "It took a lot of guts to run," "You only get a chance at a home run if you're willing to swing the bat," "Abe Lincoln lost his first few political campaigns—he still did okay," "I'll try a few different things next time," "I'm as good as anybody else whether I won or not," "What's the worst that can happen from this?"

Parent: You get a bad grade in math, and a thought comes that says, "I'm a bad student. I must be dumb." Give me a few Thought Chops.

Child: "I can do a Solution Time with Mom and figure out what I need to do," "I can do better if I try harder and get some help," "People are born with different talents—mine isn't math, but I'm great at other things."

Parent: You go to a school party and some older kids in a group laugh and point at you, and a thought comes that says, "I must be a geek or something." Give me a few Thought Chops.

Child: "Who cares? I'll just shrug them off," "I'm as good as anybody else on the planet, especially those guys," "I have no idea what they're doing, and who cares?"

Remember when you have bad feelings to use Thought Chops to talk back to false beliefs and thinking mistakes.

Usually children just need an understanding ear and heart. It's healthy for them to own and experience their feelings, and they don't need us to do anything except give them our full (mindful) attention and listen without interruption. But sometimes they may want or need our help. We shouldn't minimize their feelings when they experience difficult events, but we can help them get perspective. As difficult events happen in your children's lives, help them to come up with Thought Chops that reinforce the notion that bad events are temporary, isolated, and not to be taken too personally. Bad events happen to everybody, and your children remain as good as anybody else, even if they have to go through difficult experiences.

Model Thought Chops out loud when you're around your children and you're dealing with a setback or an undesired event.

Coaching Tools to Help Children Counter Self-defeating Thoughts

Questions to Help Uncover Self-defeating Beliefs and Thoughts

We need to keep an eye out toward helping our children change any self-defeating core beliefs they have. Core beliefs are what people fundamentally believe about themselves and about the world. People have core beliefs about their goodness, their worth, and their competence. These core beliefs are like blueprints. They strongly influence our everyday attitudes, assumptions, thoughts, feelings, and actions. They provide us with our rules for living. Even though they're only ideas, we automatically consider these core beliefs true—just the way things "are." We discount evidence that contradicts these beliefs, and we glom onto evidence that supports them. Self-defeating core beliefs are rigid and overgeneralized, and they usually come in forms like these: "I'm bad," "I'm unworthy," "I'm defective," "I'm powerless," "I'm unlovable." We need to consciously strive to notice and understand our children's core beliefs about themselves and the world. If they have self-defeating beliefs, we need to help them adopt new beliefs. The beliefs that we help to instill in them will be part of their blueprints in life.

Beliefs come from information that we receive and accept. People believed that the earth was flat until they received new information and accepted it. In the same way, if our children believe that they're fundamentally not good, we need to keep giving them new information in a form they can truly accept and believe. One of the best ways of determining whether our children have self-defeating core beliefs about themselves or the world is to probe them lightly with key questions when they're undergoing difficult emotional situations and are willing to talk. Questions like "Why would that be bad?" "What would that mean?" and "What's the worst that would happen if that were true?" can be helpful in getting to core beliefs. Continue to ask these questions, as well as the simple question "Why?", until you arrive at some core beliefs. You know that you've hit core self-defeating beliefs when your kids provide statements about themselves that take these forms: (1) "I'm bad" beliefs ("I'm defective," "I'm unattractive," "I'm unwanted") or (2) "I'm helpless" beliefs ("I'm a failure," "I'm incompetent," "I'm inadequate," "I'm weak"). Once we get to self-defeating core beliefs, we can give our children logic, evidence, examples, and new phrases to help them counter the self-defeating beliefs and ultimately adopt new beliefs. We do this by both verbally contradicting the self-defeating beliefs and putting a halt to any of the everyday attitudes, criticisms, and opinions we express that might be subversively supporting those beliefs. Often the only thing supporting these beliefs are distorted ideas that children have simply learned to accept. My favorite question in challenging these beliefs is "Who made that rule?" Some of the cognitive therapy books in the reading list provide helpful, detailed tools that can be used to help children create new, more realistic core beliefs.

The following types of simple questions may also be beneficial in helping kids through times when their bad feelings become especially troublesome. I've found that perceptions and generalizations can make events seem much worse for children than they really are. When you help them look at the details more realistically, their bad feelings can begin to melt away.

When Kids Feel Fear or Worry

First Questions: Are you afraid or worried about something? What thing?

Probing for Thinking Mistakes: How bad would it actually be? (Exaggerating). How do you know it will be bad? (Jumping to Conclusions). Are all parts of it bad? (All-or-Nothing Thinking). Are there other ways of looking at it? (go through the But Twist). Can we come up with ideas that would deal with whatever makes you afraid or worried? (do Solution Time).

Probing for Self-defeating Beliefs: Are you afraid or worried about what people will think of you? If people thought poorly of you or made fun of you, what would that mean? Do you think people are bad if others think poorly of them or make fun of them? (Why? Who made that rule?)

Taking Action: Give evidence and real-life examples of why these are false beliefs. Come up with Thought Chops together that can be used in similar future situations.

When Kids Feel Helplessness

First Questions: Are you feeling like you just can't do something because it's too hard and not fun? What thing? What's hard about it?

Probing for Thinking Mistakes: Is it really as hard as you think? (Exaggerating). How do you know it will be that hard? (Jumping to Conclusions). Are all parts of it hard? (All-or-Nothing Thinking). Are there parts of it that could even be fun, or at least not too bad? (Focusing on the Bad). Are there other ways of looking at this? (Go through the But Twist). Can we come up with a plan to get this done in a way that won't make it seem so hard? (do Solution Time).

Probing for Self-defeating Beliefs: Do you believe that everything that humans need to do should be easy and fun? (Why? What does real life teach us?) Do you think people can't be happy if they have to do something hard? (Why?) Do you think hard things are bad? (Why?) Do you think if people don't always do their best, it's bad? (Why?). What would it mean if you tried something that was hard and you failed?

Taking Action: Give evidence and real-life examples of why these are false beliefs. Come up with Thought Chops together that can be used in similar future situations.

When Kids Feel Guilt

First Questions: Do you feel bad because of something you did or didn't do? What did you do? Do you feel like that makes you bad?

Probing for Thinking Mistakes: Why is what you did really that bad? (Exaggerating). Is everything about the experience bad? (All-or-Nothing Thinking). Why do you think you're so responsible for what happened? (Blaming Ourselves). Can we come up with ideas that can make up for what happened? Can we figure out a time limit to your feeling bad? (do Solution Time). Do you think that what happened makes you bad? (Labeling). Are there other ways of looking at this? (go through the But Twist).

Probing for Self-defeating Beliefs: Do you believe people shouldn't make mistakes? (Why? What does real life teach us?) Do you believe people are bad if they make mistakes? (Why? Who made that rule?) Do you believe people are bad if others say they're bad? (Why?) What would it mean if you made a mistake or had a bad thing happen?

Taking Action: Give evidence and real-life examples of

why these are false beliefs. Come up with Thought Chops together that can be used in similar future situations.

When Kids Feel Rejection

First Questions: Do you feel bad because somebody doesn't like you? Who doesn't like you? What exactly did they do or say?

Probing for Thinking Mistakes: Why are you so sure they don't like you? (Jumping to Conclusions). Doesn't anybody like you? (All-or-Nothing Thinking). Do you think that in fact sometimes to be yourself it might even be good to not be liked? (Focusing on the Bad).

Probing for Self-defeating Beliefs: Do you believe that all people in the world like each other? (Why? What does real life teach us?) Do you believe people are bad if they're not liked? (Why? Who made that rule?) Do you think people have to be liked to be happy? (Why?) Do you think people need to be good-looking, have money, and be popular to be happy? (Why?) If somebody didn't like you, what would that mean?

Taking Action: Give evidence and real-life examples of why these are false beliefs. Come up with Thought Chops together that can be used in similar future situations.

When Kids Feel Anger or Hurt

First Questions: Are you feeling angry or hurt about something somebody did to you or said to you? What exactly did they do or say?

Probing for Thinking Mistakes: Are you absolutely sure that they said or did these things—or do you just suppose they did, or maybe it was just told to you? (Jumping to Conclusions). Is what they said or did really that bad? (Exaggerating). Do you think they're completely bad because they did this? (Labeling). Do you think they need to make up for what they said or did? Do you need to talk to them directly about this? (do Solution Time).

Probing for Self-defeating Beliefs: Do you believe people are bad or weak if others do hurtful things to them? (Why? What does real life teach us?) Do you think that what people say about us must be true, just because they say it? (Why?) If somebody were to say a mean thing to you, what would that mean?

Taking Action: Give evidence and real-life examples of why these are false beliefs. Come up with Thought Chops together that can be used in similar future situations.

First Questions: Are you feeling angry or hurt because you can't have what you want? What do you want?

Probing for Thinking Mistakes: How bad is it really for you not to get exactly what you want? What's the worst thing that will happen if you don't get it? (Exaggerating, Focusing on the Bad, Jumping to Conclusions). Can you get something a little different than the exact thing you want? (All-or-Nothing Thinking). Are there other ways of looking at this? (go through the But Twist). If this is something you really need to have, can we figure out a plan to get it? (do Solution Time).

Probing for Self-defeating Beliefs: Do you believe people always need to get what they want in life? (Why? What does real life tell us?) Do you believe people always have to get what they want in order to be happy? (Who made that rule?) If you didn't get what you wanted, what would that mean?

Taking Action: Give evidence and real-life examples of why these are false beliefs. Come up with Thought Chops together that can be used in similar future situations.

When Kids Feel Sadness

First Questions: Are you feeling sad because something bad happened? What exactly happened?

Probing for Thinking Mistakes: How bad is what happened? (Exaggerating). Was the whole thing bad? (All-or-Nothing Thinking). Do you feel like you're responsible for what happened? (Blaming Ourselves). Are there other ways of looking at this? (go through the But Twist). Can we do something to change what happened? (do Solution Time).

Probing for Self-defeating Beliefs: Do you believe that bad things don't happen to people? (Why? What does real life tell us?) Do you believe that bad things shouldn't happen to you? (Why?) Do you believe people can't eventually be happy again after bad things happen to them?

Taking Action: Give evidence and real-life examples of why these are false beliefs. Come up with Thought Chops together that can be used in similar future situations.

First Questions: Do you feel sad because you think

somebody is better than you or has something better than what you have? Why are they better? What do they have that's better?

Probing for Thinking Mistakes: How much better do you think they are? How much better is what they have? (Exaggerating). Are they better at everything? Is everything they have better? (All-or-Nothing Thinking).

Probing for Self-defeating Beliefs: Do you believe that some people are better than others if they have better things, look better, or can do things better? (Why? Who made that rule?) What would it mean if somebody was better than you at something or had better things?

Taking Action: Give evidence and real-life examples of why these are false beliefs. Come up with Thought Chops together that can be used in similar future situations.

Remember that the ultimate goal of the questioning process is to help your children see the unreasonableness of dysfunctional thinking and beliefs. Such coaching conversations are more art than science and aren't always linear in nature. The basic sequence is to identify the events that have triggered the bad feelings, deal with thinking mistakes, uncover and counter any self-defeating core beliefs that are driving the whole thing, and create useful Thought Chops. Here are some examples of how these conversations might flow:

Parent: Do you feel bad because of something that somebody did?

Child: Yeah, some kids were laughing at me at school.

Parent: What were they laughing about exactly?

Child: I don't know—they were just mean and I don't like them.

Parent: Do you think you're bad if people laugh at you?

Child: No, I just think they're mean.

Parent: Do you think that people aren't ever mean in life?

Child: Well, they shouldn't be.

Parent: Would you agree that they shouldn't be, but sometimes they are?

Child: Yeah.

Parent: What can you do when they're mean to you?

Child: I don't know.

Parent: Can you use the Power I, the Shrug, or the Disappearing Act?

Child: Maybe.

Parent: Do you think that people aren't as good if others laugh at them?

Child: Maybe a little bit.

Parent: Do you think Abraham Lincoln wasn't good because a lot of people made fun of him and laughed at him?

Child: No.

Parent: Remember, that just like Abraham Lincoln, you're a normal, worthwhile human no matter what. If people make fun of you, that's their problem, not yours. Are there other Thought Chops that you could use in this type of situation? Also remember to use the Power I, the Shrug, or the Disappearing Act if this happens again.

Another example:

Parent: You feel bad because you didn't have a great piano recital?

Child: Yeah, I totally messed up.

Parent: Did you mess up every note or just a few notes?

Child: I messed up just a couple, but it was terrible.

Parent: Do you think that people don't ever make mistakes?

Child: They make mistakes, but this was really bad.

Parent: What's the worst that can happen if you make mistakes?

Child: Everybody will think I'm a dork.

Parent: I think you're exaggerating a little bit, but what's the worst thing that can happen if everybody did think that?

Child: It would just be bad.

Parent: But what's the worst thing that would actually happen to you?

Child: Well, not a whole lot.

Parent: Do you think people aren't as good if they make mistakes?

Child: Sort of.

Parent: Who made that rule?

Child: I don't know.

Parent: Well, it's not a rule, because every human on this planet makes mistakes sometimes. Part of being a normal human is to make mistakes.

Child: Maybe, but I still feel bad.

Parent: It's normal to feel bad if this happens, but just remember that even the best musicians in the world make mistakes sometimes. These things happen to everybody. What other Thought Chops could you use if this happens in the future?

Examples of Written Responses to Self-defeating Beliefs and Thoughts

It might be helpful for you and your child to sit down with pen and paper and more formally and precisely identify your child's self-defeating beliefs or thinking errors. Then you can write out good responses that your child can use when those thoughts come up. (A good resource for this process is David Burns's book *Feeling Good.*) Experiment with logical responses until you come upon that one "aha!" response that really helps your child see the light in terms that he or she can believe. Here are some examples of this written process:

Self-Defeating Belief or Thinking Mistakes	Examples of Thought Chops
Your child generally feels like he's bad if people make fun of him.	• Some people laughed at Michael Jordan on the basketball court. Did that somehow make him bad? • If I laugh at a mountain, does that somehow magically change the mountain and make it bad? • What verbal technique can I use the next time someone laughs at me? What kind of funny Reverse Tease could I use? • Some people with geeky habits laugh at others all the time—why would I care about their opinion? • I'm as good as anybody else no matter what—so what does it matter if somebody laughs at me? • What's the worst thing that can happen to me if someone laughs at me?
Your child is afraid to act in a play because she might make a mistake. She generally believes that it's bad to make mistakes and have people laugh at you.	• Everybody makes mistakes sometimes. • Even the best actors in the world make mistakes in a play. If I do make a mistake, that's completely normal.

- It takes a lot of guts just to get up there. A lot more guts than just sitting out in the audience.
- If I do make a mistake, I can just make up some lines and get the general idea across. All the words don't have to be perfect.
- No matter what happens, I remain as good as anybody else. Mistakes can't magically make a person bad. Mistakes are a normal part of being human.
- I can keep notes in my pocket or on my hand to remind me if I forget something.
- What's the worst thing that will happen if I make mistakes?
- You can get a hit only if you're willing to swing the bat.
- Who made the rule that people aren't good if they make mistakes?

Your child is angry because he can't go to a basketball camp he wanted to go to. He generally believes that he needs to get what he wants to be happy.

- I'll get over it.
- Michael Jordan didn't go to basketball camps, and he still learned to play basketball pretty well.
- I'll spend a little more time just practicing on the courts on my own.

	• You can't have everything you want. • Feeling good and tough inside doesn't come from what you get; it comes from good, tough thinking. • What's the worst thing that will happen if I don't go?
Your child is having a hard time in her PE class, and she's starting to feel inadequate and inferior about it.	• I'm as good as anybody else on the planet. • Everybody has different talents. • PE really isn't all that important. I'll try, but I don't have to be an Olympic star. • What's the worst thing that can happen if I'm not a star in PE? • I'll just relax and try to have more fun with it. • Who made the rule that people who run faster are better?

When, despite your best efforts, your child feels bad too often, too intensely, and for too long, make sure to get help from a professional counselor. Changing beliefs and ways of thinking isn't easy for anyone, and professional coaching can't hurt. Remember that whatever type of counseling you seek, the counselor's toolbox should include effective ways of ultimately changing dysfunctional core beliefs.

CHAPTER SEVEN

The Way of the Hawk: Practicing Mindfulness

Hawks are universal symbols for paying attention. They sit for hours in dignified, calm stillness, then glide gracefully across the skies, vigilant for prey. We're told that their eyesight is probably eight times as powerful as our own. When we hear of someone with the eyes of a hawk, we think of a person who is acutely alert and perceptive. The Way of the Hawk is the way of calmly paying attention.

One of the basic principles of the martial arts is to achieve clear mental awareness and calmness. As far back as the early sixth century of the common era, Bodhidharma, an Indian priest and knight, carried with him to China both mindfulness techniques (from Buddhism) and a system of martial arts (the early forms of jujitsu). Clearly these tools were meant to go hand in hand. When the martial arts are performed mindfully, practitioners are better able to reach their full potential. Paired with clear, calm mental focus and a concentrated awareness, the movements of the martial arts become more natural and fluid.

So, too, the verbal techniques in this book are more effective if you are calmly aware of what's going on in the present moment. We all know that kids and calmness often don't go together. Kids get excited. Just go to the playground of any elementary school in America, and you'll see a wonderful scene of little humans wrestling, tussling, running, screaming, climbing, yelling, and pulling. By nature, kids all have "ants in their pants." That's a wonderful childlike quality, but sometimes it can spin out to a loss of control. And which of us hasn't found ourselves locked into the escalating parental mantra of "Settle down . . . calm down . . . I mean it! . . . time out! . . . *Hey, knock it off!*"? By enhancing a child's ability (and your own) to calm down and pay attention in a nonjudgmental manner, you can improve his or her ability to respond to challenging situations.

Another potential benefit of mindfulness can last a lifetime. By learning to be calmly aware in the present moment, children have a better chance of hanging on to one of the most magical aspects of childhood—wonder, the ability to fully enjoy and appreciate the *here* and *now*—as they develop into adults.

It can be very difficult for children to have the patience to pay attention calmly. It may also be difficult for them to separate their thoughts and their feelings from themselves. To live mindfully means to begin not to take thoughts and feelings so personally, to be fully aware of them but to see them more as sensations. It means to relax the impulse to judge our thoughts, feelings, or anything else. Sometimes it's hard to relax and let go of troublesome feelings until we deal with the false beliefs and thinking mistakes that might be behind them. Helping your child to develop helpful Thought Chops can help him or her to relax and let go.

The paradox is that achieving calm awareness requires some real effort if kids aren't used to it, and they may require adult-level consciousness to fully understand and develop it as a part of their lives. The practices that are included in the Way of the Hawk are therefore not meant to train children formally in mindfulness but simply to give them a taste of what it's like to be fully and calmly aware and relaxed in the present moment. These practices show them what mindfulness is like. Once your kids understand these mindfulness tools, they can serve as examples of how to pay attention and calm down. The full benefit of these examples may not come into play until your children are adults and can pursue this practice on their own more formally. As adults they may also better comprehend and deal with thoughts and feelings as "things" or sensations that are separate from themselves—as opposed to believing that they are those thoughts and feelings. I have personally found meditation—a form of mindfulness—very helpful in calming my mind. No matter how hectic my life is, it's something I strive to do every day (even if it's only during my commute or lunchtime walk).

It can be very difficult for children to have the patience to pay attention calmly. The mindfulness practices give them a taste of what it's like to be calmly aware and relaxed in the present moment.

SCRIPT TO INTRODUCE THE WAY OF THE HAWK

Hawks are good examples in nature of calmly paying attention. Sometimes you can see them sitting on telephone lines, watching the fields below, waiting to catch a mouse or other prey. They just sit and wait, sometimes for hours. Their eyesight is probably eight times as powerful as our own, so they can see lots of things while they wait. The Way of the Hawk is the way of calmly paying attention.

When martial arts were introduced to China from India a long time ago, they were taught along with something called mindfulness. Mindfulness means calmly paying attention to what's happening in the present moment and letting go of other thoughts and feelings. This practice can help you do things better and enjoy life more.

For example, if you're playing basketball but you start worrying about missing shots, you probably won't play as well or have as much fun. Or if you're licking an ice cream cone but thinking about homework, you can't enjoy the ice cream cone as much. Or if you're doing your chores but thinking about how much you'd rather be doing something else, the chores can seem much harder than they really are.

Part of mindfulness is letting go of thoughts that bother us. Letting go of thoughts is something we do all the time. In one moment you might let go of a thought about doing homework and move to a thought about getting a snack. In another moment, you might let go of a thought about talking on the telephone and move to a thought about watching TV. Sometimes you might let go of angry thoughts and move to happy thoughts. Mindfulness means to let go of all our busy thoughts and cares and calmly pay attention to what's happening in the present moment.

Another important part of mindfulness is not to make judgments about what's going on. This means that you don't think so much about what you dislike about things—you just calmly notice them. We can waste a lot of time deciding what we don't like about other people, about the world, about the weather, about school or work, about how we look, about mistakes we've made or others have made, and many other things. With mindfulness we try to notice and understand what things are like and let go of thoughts about what we don't like about them.

The Way of the Hawk is made up of five practices that

give examples of what this calm paying attention, or mindfulness, is like.

Mindfulness Practice 1: Mindful Eating

A very simple way to introduce the concept of mindfulness, or calmly and nonjudgmentally paying attention, is to show children Mindful Eating. Mindful Eating means really paying attention to the details of eating as you eat. It can be taught with any food or drink. For example, give your child a cookie. Tell your child that instead of eating it in the usual, automatic way, he or she should pay close attention to the detail of the taste of the cookie and where that taste occurs in the mouth; to the way the cheeks, tongue, teeth, and throat work in concert to break down and digest the cookie; to the texture of the cookie in the mouth. The child learns to eat or drink and actually *experience* eating or drinking by paying close attention to what's happening in the process. Mindful Eating can become a reference point for other training related to achieving calm focus. The concept of mindfulness is always similar, regardless of the particular application—it always involves calmly paying attention to what's happening in the present moment in a nonjudgmental manner. Mindful Eating is a good place to start.

Sometimes at mealtime, just as a fun thing to do, I'll ask my children to close their eyes and tell me what they notice when they eat or drink something, and I do the same thing. We also do "taste tests" as a fun way to have a similar experience.

Script to Introduce Mindful Eating

Let's begin learning the Way of the Hawk with something called Mindful Eating. A lot of times we just eat and don't take the time to enjoy it. Mindful Eating means that we're going to eat some things together, and we're going to really pay attention to what the thing we're eating feels and tastes like. We're going to notice all the details. We're also not going to judge the food—we're going to concentrate on what it actually tastes like, and how it differs from other tastes, but we're not going to decide in what ways we don't like it. If other thoughts or distractions come into your mind as we're eating, go ahead and notice them, don't judge them, and calmly return to just paying attention to the eating.

Practicing Mindful Eating Together

Begin by giving your children something ordinary or extraordinary to eat or drink. Sometimes ordinary things are good, because they can remind your kids of how ordinary things can be quite extraordinary when you simply become aware of them.

Have your children close their eyes, slowly feel the food in their mouths, and pay attention to the details of their eating experience.

You go through the experience at the same time—eating the same food and paying attention with them.

To help them pay attention, ask questions that will keep your kids focused. For example, "What is the taste really like?" "What part of your teeth first bites down on the food?" "How do you move the food around inside your mouth?" "Where exactly do you first start to taste the food?" and so on. To experience eating in this mindful manner can provide some fun surprises for both you and your children.

As they eat, remind your kids that if any other thoughts or feelings enter their minds, they should just gently let them go and return to paying attention to the details of their eating.

Repeat the experience every so often with different types of foods or drinks. Have your children notice how the experience is different with different types of foods or drinks. Maybe every so often have an entire "mindful" sit-down meal together.

Mindfulness Practice 2: Balloon Belly

Like Mindful Eating, Balloon Belly is a technique for helping train children to calmly pay attention. In this case they are learning to pay attention to their breathing—or learning mindful breathing. One of life's great, unnoticed, everyday wonders is the unceasing ebb and flow of our own breathing. It reminds us of the soothing rhythm of waves on the ocean or on a large inland lake. By learning to simply sit and breathe, gently noticing and letting go of other thoughts and cares as they try to intrude, we not only learn to relax our minds but also begin to learn the simple art of being. We start to experience how to center ourselves in a state of peaceful stillness. By teaching our children to use their own breathing as an object of mindful focus, we give them a tool that they can take with them anywhere to help bring them back into calm focus.

I'll occasionally do a brief, informal Balloon Belly with my kids at night before we have a good-night prayer. They sometimes giggle their way through it, but that's part of the fun.

Script to Introduce the Balloon Belly

Another way to practice calmly paying attention is called Balloon Belly. Balloon Belly is like Mindful Eating, but instead of paying attention to what we're eating, we pay attention to our breathing.

We hardly ever pay attention to our breathing, but it's always there. When you do pay attention to it, you're reminded that there's a constant inflow and outflow of air going on right under your nose. It's like the waves of the ocean or a big lake. The waves never stop flowing in and flowing out, which can be quite peaceful and soothing.

To practice Balloon Belly, we're going to sit or lie down and just calmly pay attention to our breathing. It's okay if other thoughts or feelings come that distract you from your breathing. Just notice them for a moment, don't judge them, and then go back to noticing your breathing. This practice is called Balloon Belly because our bellies blow up and then deflate like a balloon when we breathe. In fact, one good way to pay attention to our breathing is to notice the movement of our bellies. Sometimes it's nice just to put your hands on your belly and notice how it goes up and down as you breathe.

Practicing the Balloon Belly Together

Have your child sit or lie down in a comfortable position.

Instruct your child to begin to pay attention to his or

her breathing. This doesn't mean to think about breathing but simply to notice the breathing. Your child should notice the feel of the fresh air going through his or her mouth or nostrils as he or she inhales—the feel of the air gently touching the roof of the mouth and the back of the throat as it winds its way down to the esophagus. Encourage your child to notice the sound of his or her breath, both inhaling and exhaling.

To help your child pay attention—and appreciate the full meaning of the balloon metaphor—he or she should place both hands on his or her belly and feel how the belly expands on the inhale and recedes on the exhale.

As your child practices, just remind him or her to gently let go of any feelings of boredom, irritation, or worry (or any other thoughts or feelings) and return to paying attention to the movement of the belly and the overall experience of breathing. If his or her mind drifts away twenty times from the breathing, he or she should simply make note of that and return to the breathing twenty times.

It's important that your child understand that he or she isn't trying to breathe in a special way. The goal here is just to notice the breathing.

Practice with your child a few minutes at a time, anytime you care to. The idea is to introduce him or her casually to mindfulness and to achieving greater calmness through just breathing, noticing breathing, and letting go of everything else.

Mindfulness Practice 3: Sky Watching

For many of us there's nothing quite as calming as simply sitting (or lying) in a field or on the patio and watching a bright blue sky dotted with clouds during the day or a starry sky at night. With Sky Watching, the focus is on watching the sky and the out-of-doors while paying attention to what our other senses are able to pick up: the sights of clouds and birds, the feel of the wind, the heat of the sun, the sounds of nature and human activity, and so forth. If other thoughts or feelings come, we let them drift away by returning our attention to calmly watching the sky and noticing the other sensations of the moment. While doing Sky Watching, we become like mountains—sitting or lying calm and relaxed, a part of nature. But as humans we are fortunate enough also to be observers of nature.

As in Mindful Eating, where we pay attention to eating, and Balloon Belly, where we pay attention to breathing, in Sky Watching we're paying attention to the often overlooked. Now, though, we've widened the scope to the much larger "moment"—the whole of the sky and other visual surroundings and out-of-door sensations. Casually practicing these methods with our children from time to time can introduce them to the more general practice of being mindfully aware and involved in life on a calm, nonjudgmental basis.

As you've probably done, when I'm out in nature with my children, every so often I'll just stop and have us notice the sights, smells, and sounds of the moment.

Script to Introduce Sky Watching

One of the funnest things to do to learn mindfulness is just to go out, lie down, and watch the sky. Whether it's a bright blue sky, a cloudy sky, or a night sky, there's always something to see, if you just relax and watch calmly. To practice this, we're going to go outside, lie down, and relax as we watch the sky. I want you also to notice the sounds, smells, and any other sights that you become aware of. If your mind drifts away and you start thinking about worries or being bored, just let go of those thoughts and return to relaxing calmly. Every so often you and I should just go out and watch the sky together—so you remind me if we haven't done it for a while.

Practicing Sky Watching Together

You might have your kids start with the Balloon Belly just to get into a calm mode, but this isn't necessary.

Point out some details to help keep them, and yourself, focused. For example, you can notice clouds (or stars at night), or jets, or birds, or trees, or hills, or the feel of wind, or the heat of the sun, or the sound of a motorcycle, or the call of a bird, or the bark of a dog, or whatever else is happening.

Remind your kids that if other thoughts come, they should simply let them float away as they return to watching the sky and the out-of-doors.

Mostly, though, you just want to sit or lie there and simply enjoy the sense of being, doing nothing except watching the sky and the out-of-doors. Nothing at all needs to be said or done.

Mindfulness Practice 4: The Rock

The Rock is another technique that can be quite fun to practice. The Rock is *doing* things mindfully—just doing and letting go of thought. You practice this by simply tossing a beanbag or shooting basketballs. While the children are making their attempts, you should try to distract them by waving your arms, telling a funny joke, or doing something else distracting. The object of this practice is to have the children let go of any concerns about whether they make the shots, how to handle the distractions, or any other thoughts. They should simply toss or shoot. This is all about letting go, especially of any "I can't" thoughts or any cares about either making or missing tosses or shots. This is a practice in calmly doing and letting go of distracting thoughts while in the process of physical activity. In the future, when your children say they can't do something, you can ask them just to do, not to think about it, just like when they practiced the Rock.

My children have become so accustomed to the Rock as a game that sometimes they'll go out and play it on their own by one of them shooting free throws while the other tries to provide a major distraction (just like the fans do in a pro basketball game).

Script to Introduce the Rock

Another fun practice for learning mindfulness is called the Rock. With the Rock we're going to play some simple games and you're going to practice not being distracted by thoughts or by the things around you. There are lots of examples of people who do the Rock in real life:

Michelle Kwan when she ice-skates, Tiger Woods when he putts a golf ball, and Steffi Graf when she plays tennis. Many scientists, doctors, and other people have also learned to calmly pay attention to what they're doing—letting go of their cares and worries.

To do the Rock, I'm going to put this box at the other side of the room, and you're going to just practice tossing this ball into the box. As you do that, I'm going to try to distract you. I might try to make you laugh, or I might wave my arms or something else, but I just want you to keep tossing the balls. It's important not to even care if you make it or miss it, just to keep focused on tossing and not paying attention to me as best you can. In real life, when you need or want to do things that might not be fun or easy, you can practice the Rock by letting go of any "I can't" thoughts or other distractions that come up.

Practicing the Rock Together

Put a box several feet away and give your children beanbags, Nerf balls, rolled up newspapers, or other items that they can toss. Have them practice tossing the items into the box without thought or concern. Just as in learning mindful breathing, have them pay attention to tossing the items into the box and letting go of other thoughts. Encourage them not to care whether they make the shot or miss, just to calmly keep trying. Then try distracting them by waving your arms, making faces, telling a joke, or making a loud noise. Have them continue to calmly focus.

Do the same with shooting basketballs, tossing horseshoes, putting with a golf club (à la Tiger Woods), or any other such practice.

Over time, have your kids try doing the Rock with more difficult endeavors: homework, piano practice, and so on.

In everyday life, when your children use "can't do" language, refer to the Rock. Tell them just to do what they need to do, letting go of all thoughts and concerns, just like with the Rock.

Mindfulness Practice 5: Mindful Chores

This final mindfulness practice is another *doing* practice. One of the best ways that children can overcome "I can't" thoughts is to have lots of practice in *doing*. As they learn that they really *can* do things, even things that aren't fun and easy, "I can't" thoughts will have less power in their lives. In earlier times children had plenty of practice doing things. As part of the family unit of production, they were required to participate in growing food or running a cottage industry. While for most of us today there are not as many chances for these types of "chores," there are still plenty of opportunities. Parents can help their children develop greater self-discipline and a sense that they can get things done by providing them with chores. Chores can include washing dishes, housecleaning, doing yard work, making beds, caring for pets, running errands, playing a musical instrument, and doing schoolwork. Chores give children the opportunity to practice the Rock, the But Twist, and other techniques. Children can strengthen their "I can" thinking further by doing their chores mindfully. Mindful Chores means doing chores while calmly paying attention to the details of the activity in the present moment, in the same spirit as Mindful Eating and Balloon Belly. It means noticing the details of the chores as they're being done. It also means noticing the thoughts and feelings that come as your kids are doing chores and simply letting go of those thoughts as they return to calmly doing their chores. This practice can generate greater patience, acceptance, and nonjudgment of the chores as they're being done.

Script to Introduce Mindful Chores

Another mindfulness practice is called Mindful Chores. Mindful Chores is like the Rock, except instead of doing a simple tossing game we do chores. We calmly pay attention to the details of our chores as we're doing them, and let go of other thoughts. Chores aren't usually nearly as bad as our thoughts can make them out to be. In fact, some aspects of chores can be enjoyable if we learn simply to pay attention to the present moment, rather than only think about what we don't like and what we'll do when we're through. For example, if the chore is washing dishes, we can be mindful of the temperature of the water, of the feel of scrubbing, of carefully placing the dishes in the dishwasher, of the smell of the detergent. If the chore is pulling weeds, we can be mindful of the texture of the weeds, the feel of the dirt, the heat from the sun, and so forth. The chore may still not be fun to us, but it won't seem as bad if we simply do it and let go of irritating thoughts.

Practicing Mindful Chores Together

Together, write down or reconfirm the chores that your child is responsible for.

Make the time to follow up on these chores. It's particularly important to do some of the chores together and make the process more enjoyable by pointing out and paying attention to the details. This is also a great time just to be together and talk to your children.

Some Closing Thoughts

The main point of *Sticks and Stones* is to provide you with a relatively easy way to give your children the tools they need to counter hurtful words that others tell them and that they tell themselves. It's also meant to help them to be verbally sociable and kind. I believe that some of these tools can help children to be happy and to do good. But I also hope this book will prompt you to think about whether you're awake to your children and their needs. I hope the exercises will provide another excuse for discussion and interaction with your children. None of us are perfect parents, and we don't need to be. Nature doesn't require perfect parenting for kids to develop in healthy ways, as long as our parenting is "good enough." In fact too much parental doting and control present their own problems. But our kids do need our protection, our training, and our unconditional love. We all "doze off" sometimes when it comes to our children—it's only natural. But if we remain in a state of perpetual slumber when it comes to looking out for their well-being and developing close relationships with then, we'll miss out on some of the most important and enjoyable aspects of our human experience.

As I was finishing this book my fourteen-year-old niece, Katie, was killed in an automobile accident. She was close to my own family, and it's been very painful to be separated from her. She was, and is, a wonderful girl. Fortunately, my brother and sister-in-law lived their family life in such a way that they were able to appreciate and enjoy their experience with Katie to the fullest. Their home has always been filled with love, warmth, and fun. I'm humbled by their examples as parents who raised their daughter in ways that they would never have to regret. But this tragedy has reminded me that none of us know how long our experience with our children (or nieces, nephews, and other loved ones) will be. We can't take our time with them for granted.

By choosing to become parents, you and I signed on to love and care for our children. Sometimes, if we're not careful, we can unintentionally give this major responsibility short shrift. As the world has grown ever more complex and bewildering, we parents have turned over so much of the training and care of our children to others. Schools, sports leagues, day-care centers, churches, the government, and other institutions can certainly play a supporting role in teaching and training our children. But for those of us who've made the parenting choice, raising a child isn't a job, it's part of the basic fabric of life. It's not simply a means to something else, it's one of the fundamental purposes of life itself.

It's especially important to look inside ourselves and see if we've fallen into any of the habits of poor thinking that were described in the last chapter. Namely, have we allowed ourselves to develop detrimental habits of exaggerating, focusing on the bad, all-or-nothing thinking, labeling, jumping to conclusions, or blaming when it comes to our children? If we're not careful, we can develop distorted views of our children that affect how we feel toward them. We need to be understanding, patient, and accepting of them as they travel through their various stages of development. Why should we expect our small children and teenagers to act like adults when they're not?

We also need to fact the reality of our times and more consciously oversee the mentoring of our children. When people lived in small tribes, it was clear that parents needed to take responsibility for the training of their children. If they didn't, who else would? A parent's job wasn't finished until his or her children were prepared to survive in the world. Parents and children worked and played shoulder to shoulder, so the mentoring took place in a fairly natural, on-the-job kind of way. Up until the early 1900s, 90 percent of all fathers worked at home (on the family farm or in home-based industries). Children learned how to become adults from the adults around them, not from other children or from TV programs and movies. Now not only fathers but many mothers work away from their home and children. In such a world, institutions can be a support, but they can't provide the customized mentoring and care that children need. Somebody needs to be their guide and mentor. Somebody needs to function as their personal agent, who ensures that their well-being is looked after. What better agent could your children have than you—the person who loves them more than anything else in the world.

Helpful Readings on Mindfulness Practice and Cognitive Therapy

Beck, Judith S. *Cognitive Therapy: Basics and Beyond* (New York: Guilford Press, 1995). While this book is meant primarily for professional practitioners of cognitive therapy, it provides valuable insights into the types of approaches that are being used to help people change dysfunctional beliefs and thoughts.

Burns, David D. *Feeling Good: The New Mood Therapy* (New York: William Morrow, 1980). This book is a primer on cognitive therapy for the layperson. It's an excellent guide for becoming more aware of one's internal life.

Goldstein, Joseph, and Jack Kornfield. *Seeking the Heart of Wisdom: The Path of Insight Meditation* (Boston: Shambhala, 1987). This is a very good book on mindfulness that provides specific exercises to help cultivate awareness of body, speech, and mind. It also offers guidance on developing openness and compassion.

Hanh, Thich Nhat. *Being Peace* (Berkeley: Parallax Press, 1987); *The Miracle of Mindfulness* (Boston: Beacon Press, 1976); *Peace Is Every Step* (New York: Bantam Books, 1990). Thich Nhat Hanh is a Vietnamese Zen monk who was nominated by Martin Luther King, Jr., for the Nobel Peace Prize. He has dedicated his life to teaching mindfulness as a means to inner and world peace. He has written numerous books that touch on the many aspects of mindfulness. The books listed here are good introductions to mindfulness. My personal favorite is *Peace Is Every Step.*

Kabat-Zinn, Jon. *Full Catastrophe Living* (New York: Delta, 1990). Dr. Jon Kabat-Zinn was formerly director of the Stress Reduction Clinic at the University of Massachusetts Medical Center. This book is a comprehensive manual for the application of mindfulness in everyday living. It is now used as a text for many stress reduction programs.

———. *Wherever You Go There You Are: Mindfulness Meditation in Everyday Life* (New York: Hyperion, 1994). This little follow-up book to *Full Catastrophe Living* is a wonderful addition. It provides brief, easy access to the concepts and philosophy of mindfulness.

Kabat-Zinn, Jon, and Myla Kabat-Zinn. *Everyday Blessings: The Inner Work of Mindful Parenting* (New York: Hyperion, 1997). I only wish that this book had been around when I became a father. In my opinion it's the best book available on waking up to our children and to the blessing and challenge of being a parent.

Levine, Stephen. *A Gradual Awakening* (Garden City, NY: Anchor Books, 1989). First published in 1979, this is a very good, simple little guidebook on mindfulness. It's been used at many schools (including the Harvard Medical School) to teach about meditation and mindfulness.

Seligman, Martin E. P. *Learned Optimism: How to Change Your Mind and Your Life* (New York: Pocket Books, 1990, 1998). Martin Seligman has written several books and articles on cognitive therapy and optimism. This is a good, easy-to-read book on using cognitive therapy to harness the power of "non-negative" thinking. There's a chapter devoted to teaching optimism to children.

———. *The Optimistic Child* (New York: Houghton Mifflin, 1995). This is a great primer on helping children develop optimistic explanatory styles.

Young, Jeffrey E., and Janet S. Klosko. *Reinventing Your Life* (New York: Plume, 1994). This book is primarily intended to help adults identify and change their own dysfunctional core beliefs. However, the information is also helpful in identifying the types of beliefs and attitudes you want to protect your children from.

Master Checklist

	Understanding of Concept	Completed Practice Sessions
Way of the Blue Jay		
Power I	☐	☐
No Thanks	☐	☐
Simple Questions	☐	☐
Squeaky Wheel	☐	☐
Way of the Crow		
Mea Culpa	☐	☐
Mighty Might	☐	☐
Sorry Charlie	☐	☐
Way of the Hummingbird		
The Shrug	☐	☐
Reverse Tease	☐	☐
Disappearing Act	☐	☐
Way of the Dove		
Solution Time 1	☐	☐
Coin Toss	☐	☐
Cone of Silence	☐	☐
Way of the Blackbird		
Sherlock Holmes	☐	☐
True Confessions	☐	☐
Kind Talk	☐	☐
Way of the Owl		
But Twist	☐	☐
Solution Time 2	☐	☐
Thought Chop	☐	☐
Way of the Hawk		
Mindful Eating	☐	☐
Balloon Belly	☐	☐
Sky Watching	☐	☐
Rock	☐	☐
Mindful Chores	☐	☐

Understanding of Concept: The technique has been discussed and the child understands it.

Completed Practice Sessions: The technique has been practiced in practice sessions.

Index

About the Author

SCOTT COOPER has several years of experience in youth development, including teaching, coaching, and serving on education and drug-prevention boards. He is currently a board member of the Waugh School District in Petaluma, California, and is a coach for junior-high-level basketball. He was formerly a member of the Sonoma County Advisory Board of Drug Programs. He is a principal and CFO of an international planning and design firm. In addition to his love of coaching basketball, he enjoys hiking and birding along the Northern California coastline. He is a member of the National Audubon Society (Madrone chapter) and of the Point Reyes National Seashore Association. He lives with his wife and three children in Northern California.